30
Life Principles
Study Guide

Dr. Charles F. Stanley

THOMAS NELSON
Since 1798

Published by In Touch Ministries, Atlanta, Georgia, 30340

Original design © 2007 Thomas Nelson, Inc.

Editing, layout, and design by Gregory C. Benoit Publishing, Old Mystic, CT

Unless otherwise noted, Scripture taken from the NEW AMERICAN STANDARD BIBLE, © 1960,
1962, 1963, 1968, 1971, 1972, 1973, 1975, 1977, 1995 by The Lockman Foundation.
Used by permission.

ISBN 13: 978-1-4185-3108-9

Printed in the United States of America.

12 13 14   QG   21 20 19

Karen Booze

Contents

∞

Introduction

In His Word, God has given you hundreds of life principles to help you become everything that He designed you to be. These are the tenets of faith that have been tried and proven throughout history—truths from the Bible that have never failed and will never disappoint. You can see their impact on the lives of the saints—from Old Testament times to the present day—and God has promised that, if you follow His commands, He will bless your obedience.

During his 50 years of ministry, Dr. Charles Stanley has faithfully highlighted the 30 Life Principles that have guided his life and helped him to grow in his knowledge, service, and love of God. Dr. Stanley has taught them so that others can grow into mature followers of the Lord Jesus Christ. Perhaps you've been inspired by these 30 Life Principles and are wondering how you can further make them a part of your life. What does the Bible teach about having a lifetime of spiritual success and avoiding the traps of ineffectiveness and spiritual misery? How do these Life Principles apply to your everyday circumstances and the challenges that you face?

This *30 Life Principles Study Guide* has been developed to help you answer these questions and to encourage you in growing in your relationship with Jesus Christ. Of course, these principles were never meant to take the place of God's Word. They are guidelines for discovering the richness of God's truth and knowing God Himself in a deep, intimate relationship. By following these Life Principles, you'll be on the road to the life that He designed for you. And as you submit yourself to Him more fully, God will reveal Himself to you. That's what makes the journey of obedience so exciting.

It all starts with knowing Jesus Christ as your Lord and Savior. You cannot know God without first knowing the One who reconciles you to Him. Romans 5:10 tells us, "While we were enemies we were reconciled to God through the death of His Son, much more, having been reconciled, we shall be saved by His life." God's Son, Jesus Christ, provides a relationship with Him, and He also provides eternal life if you trust Him. Romans 10:9 promises "that if you confess with your mouth Jesus as Lord, and believe in your heart that God raised Him from the dead, you will be saved."

Would you like to start a personal relationship with God, the One who created you and loves you no matter what? Tell God that you're trusting in Him for salvation. You can tell Him in your own words or use this sample prayer:

Lord Jesus, I know that Your death on the cross was enough to forgive all of my sin and restore my relationship with God. I ask You to forgive my sin and be my Savior. Thank You for providing the way for me to have a growing relationship with my heavenly Father, and thank You for giving me eternal life. I know that You hear my prayers and I praise You for loving me unconditionally and saving me. In Jesus' name, amen.

If you have just received Christ as your Savior, congratulations! You've just made the very best decision of your life! We would love to know about your decision. Please contact In Touch's Customer Care Center at (800) 789-1473, so that we can rejoice with you and send you our *New Believer's Kit* to help you take the next step in your walk with God.

Life Principle 1

Our intimacy with God—His highest priority for our lives—determines the impact of our lives.

Genesis 1:26

Life's Questions

At the beginning of any journey, you must set out in the right direction to reach your destination. That's why this study of Life Principles starts with God's wonderful purpose for bringing you into the world. To find the life that's worth living, you must understand that you're a special, beloved person and that God has a specific, wonderful plan for you that will give you all the love, fulfillment, significance, and power that you're looking for (see Rom. 12:2).

Have you wondered what motivated God to design the universe or why He created you? It was love—pure and simple. Even before the beginning of the world, God loved you and wanted to have a close, personal relationship with you that would bring great joy, fulfillment, and power to your life (see Eph. 1:4). Therefore, Life Principle 1 is: *Our intimacy with God—His highest priority for our lives—determines the impact of our lives.*

What the Bible Says

Read Genesis 1. What did God create before He formed the first man (1–25)?

Why do you think God created all of these things *before* He made people?

Why do you think it was important to God to ensure that everything was *good* (4, 10, 12, 18, 21, 25) before He created mankind (see James 1:17–18)?

—————— ∞ ——————

The word **good** in the Old Testament also means **well-pleasing**, **appealing**, **proper**, **pleasant to the senses**, **useful**, **profitable**, or **a general state of well-being and happiness**. Everything good that comes to you is from God (see James 1:17).

—————— ∞ ——————

When God said, "Let Us make man in Our image, according to Our likeness" (26), what do you think He meant? Why would He want to create someone in His image?

What jobs did God give mankind to do (26–28)?

How do our responsibilities relate to the fact that we bear His image?

───────── ∞ ─────────

The word *image* in the Old Testament also means a *likeness, model, semblance,* or *shadow.* This is what you have in common with God and why you can know Him more deeply.

───────── ∞ ─────────

What It Means

Do you wonder what God's will is for your life? He created you in His image for one reason: to have a deep, intimate relationship with Him. God created the world with everything you would ever need so that you could know and love Him. That means that nothing—ability, beauty, intelligence, money, or anything else—will ever define your life as successful in God's eyes. It all comes down to how strong your relationship is with Him.

Life Examples

Read Genesis 3. What do you suppose life was like in the garden of Eden before Adam sinned?

Why did Adam disobey God (5–6)?

In Genesis 3:10, Adam said, "I was afraid because I was naked; so I hid myself." Is there anything that you hide from God? Why are you afraid or ashamed to show that area of your life to God?

——————— ∞ ———————

When Adam and Eve covered themselves, they did so with fig leaves, which produced sap that would have greatly irritated their skin and made them even more uncomfortable and miserable.

——————— ∞ ———————

What was the punishment for Adam's sin (15–19)?

Did their lives become more or less effective after they disobeyed God?

Read John 17:1–5. Define eternal life (3).

Read 1 Corinthians 15:22. How does this verse contrast a life of separation from God with a life of intimacy with God?

Living the Principle

You were created for intimacy with God, and the difference that your relationship with God makes in your life cannot be overstated. His highest priority for you is to be involved with Him in prayer, the study of His Word, and worship and praise. Do you want to live a life that is fulfilling and significant? Do you want to make a difference in the world? Then surrender yourself completely to Jesus Christ and ask Him to open your heart to His infinite love and mercy. It's only through your fellowship and communion with God that you can truly affect other people's lives in a way that lasts eternally. Your genuine intimacy with God will become evident in every area of your life, and that will positively affect the influence that you have with every person you encounter.

How will you live out Life Principle 1 this week? Discuss ways that you can pursue a deeper relationship with God. Then spend time in prayer asking God to draw you into intimate communion with Himself and to transform your life so that you can affect the world for the sake of His kingdom.

Life Lessons to Remember

❦ *God loves you and desires your fellowship and worship* (see Deut. 6:5).

❦ *God wants your service for Him to be effective and fruitful* (see John 15:5).

❦ *God waits for you to invite Him to bless you* (see Rev. 3:20).

Life Principle 2

Obey God and leave all the consequences to Him.
Exodus 19:5

Life's Questions

How do you relate to God, His commands, and the challenges and temptations that confront you? The world denies that God has any authority, but as a believer you understand the truth. As the Creator of all that exists, God has the right and the power to conform all circumstances to His will. He's also entitled to expect a certain standard of behavior from those who believe in Him.

When God directs you to do something, how do you respond? Do His commands seem too difficult or costly for you to obey? Are you facing a decision that seems overwhelming? Are you torn about whether or not to follow God's instructions? Then Life Principle 2 should help you: *Obey God and leave all the consequences to Him.*

What the Bible Says

Read Exodus 19:1–7. What had happened to the people of Israel in Egypt? (Read Ex. 1 and Ps. 78:43–55 for a summary.)

Where were the people of Israel in this passage of Scripture (2)?

Why was it important that the Israelites saw God's power in action (4)?

---------------- ∞ ----------------

*T*he word **obey** in the Old Testament primarily means **to listen.** It can also mean to **heed, agree, consent, understand,** and **yield to.** To obey God means that you must listen for His voice and trust what He's telling you. Obeying God is absolutely essential to pleasing Him.

---------------- ∞ ----------------

What was Israel's reward if the people obeyed God (5–6)?

What does it mean to you to be God's "own possession" (5)? What especially appeals to you about the promise of His love and acceptance?

What It Means

Before Israel could take over the Promised Land, God had to teach them how to live as His people, His special possession. His commands were for their benefit and protection, so that He could establish them in the land and bless them. Their obedience was an essential part of their lives, because if they failed to observe God's laws they would face the terrible consequences of their disobedience (see Deut. 28).

The same is true for you. When you choose to disobey God, what you're really saying is that you don't have confidence in Him. Yet you cannot have intimate fellowship with someone that you don't trust. Temptations and troubles come into your life, and you worry that, if you obey God, you'll lose something that you really want. On the other hand, if you're committed to pursuing an intimate relationship with God, trusting and obeying Him in all circumstances, then you will know that you're receiving His very best for your life, which is far better than you could ever obtain on your own.

Life Examples

Read Exodus 3. What was God's command to Moses (7–10)?

What problems and consequences could come about from such a bold move by Moses (11, 13, 19; also see Ex. 4:1, 10)?

Do you think that, humanly speaking, Moses was right to be afraid with all of those obstacles? Why or why not?

What was God's specific promise to Moses (12)? How do you know that God kept His promise?

———— ∞ ————

*H*oreb and Sinai are two names for the same mountain. Some commentators think that Horeb was the western peak and Sinai was the eastern peak. Others believe that one name was for the general mountain range, while the other signified the specific mountain. Either way, we know that God kept His promise.

———— ∞ ————

Living the Principle

Exodus 19 takes place on the same mountain where God called Moses to serve Him, which means that God fulfilled His promise to His servant and to Israel. Moses obeyed God despite the consequences that confronted him. Hebrews 11:27 states, "By faith he left Egypt, not fearing the wrath of the king; for he endured, as seeing Him who is unseen." Moses trusted God, and every problem that he faced soon paled in comparison to the mighty love, wisdom, and power of the Commander.

———— ∞ ————

*I*n Exodus 3:14, God said that His name is "I AM WHO I AM." This is also translated as, "I WILL ALWAYS BE WHO I HAVE ALWAYS BEEN" or "I WILL FOREVER BE WHO I AM NOW." God never changes. As faithful and loving as He was yesterday for Moses, He will also be today, and He will continue to be for all eternity to you (see Heb. 13:8).

———— ∞ ————

So how will you live out Life Principle 2 this week? What challenge are you facing today? What is God leading you to do? Your choice in this situation will determine whether you succeed or fail; therefore, obey God and leave in His hands whatever consequence is causing you to fear. If God makes a promise to you, you can be assured that He will bring it to pass.

Spend time in prayer asking God to draw you into intimate communion with Himself, to increase your faith, and to transform your life so that you can affect the world for the sake of His kingdom.

Life Lessons to Remember

🦋 *Trust God with your life and all that concerns you* (see Prov. 3:5–6).

🦋 *Wait on the Lord for an answer to your problem or situation* (see Ps. 37:9).

🦋 *Meditate on God's Word and listen to the Holy Spirit* (see Matt. 6:33).

🦋 *Be willing to wait or walk away when the way before you is unclear* (see Ps. 27:13–14).

🦋 *Be willing to endure conflict* (see Matt. 5:10–12).

🦋 *Leave the consequences to God* (see Ex. 14:13–14).

Life Principle 3

God's Word is an immovable anchor in times of storm.
Numbers 23:19

Life's Questions

If you've made the decision to seek an intimate relationship with God and obey Him no matter what, you will undoubtedly experience seasons of difficulty and uncertainty. Your walk with God is a journey of faith, and there will be situations when your trust in Him will be tested. What will you cling to when a deluge of trouble rains on your life and everything you know to be true seems to be swept away by intense winds of adversity? What will you hold on to when the waves of doubt threaten to crash down on you? Life Principle 3 holds the answer for you: *God's Word is an immovable anchor in times of storm.*

What the Bible Says

Read Numbers 22:1–12. Why were King Balak and the Moabites afraid of the Israelites (2–5)?

Who was Balaam and what did the Moabites want from him (6–7)?

∽

The Amorites were a great deal stronger than the Moabites; so when Israel took the Amorite cities so easily (see Num. 21:21-31), the people of Moab had a good reason to be afraid.

∽

How did God respond to Balaam (12)?

Read Numbers 22:22–35. When Balaam disobeyed God, how did God get his attention (28–31)? Why do you think God used such surprising methods?

What was the angel of the Lord's specific instruction to Balaam (35)?

Read Numbers 23:16–23. Why do you think Balaam made the statement he did in Numbers 23:19?

∞

---

*W*hen Balaam said that God doesn't *lie*, it means that God will never *fail*, *deceive*, or *disappoint* you. When he says that God never has to *repent*, it's because God never changes His mind about the promises that He's made.

∞

How did God fulfill His promise to protect the people of Israel from their enemies (see Ex. 19:5; Num. 14:8–9; Josh. 24:9–10)?

What It Means

God shielded Israel from harm when the people didn't even know that they needed protecting. He caused other nations to be afraid of them and even went to unusual lengths to keep Israel from being cursed. God was so powerful and convincing that even the pagan prophet Balaam had to say, "I have received a command to bless; when He has blessed, then I cannot revoke it" (Num. 23:20).

∞

---

*T*he name *Balaam* means *not of the people*. Isn't it amazing that someone who had nothing to do with God's people could still recognize the faithfulness and power of God?

∞

God's Word is absolutely true. You may not understand how God is going to bring about what He's promised you, but He is keeping every promise that He has ever made. He will never deceive you or disappoint you, and He will never change His mind about what He's told you.

Life Examples

Read Isaiah 55:10–11. How can this passage encourage you when your situation looks bleak?

Read Romans 15:4. What does this verse mean to you?

——————— ∞ ———————

God's promises are essential to your spiritual welfare.

——————— ∞ ———————

What Scripture passages or Bible stories most encourage you? Why?

Living the Principle

Do you read and meditate on the Bible every day so that the Lord can bring His Word to your mind when you need a reminder of His love and comfort? What do you do when you're experiencing a tempest of adversity and need a special message of hope from God to hold on to? When trouble strikes like a tidal wave, God's Word can be an anchor of strength, guidance, and comfort to keep you steady.

What storm are you facing today? Are you disheartened by your situation? God will never fail you, and He'll never change His mind about the promises that He's made to you. Therefore, pray. Lay your heart out to God and ask for His love and comfort. Ask Him to show you His will and lead you to His message of encouragement. Then read His wonderful Word. A good place to find assurance is the book of Psalms; or, if you are a new believer, read the Gospel of John. Use tools such as the *Life Principles Bible* to find where in God's Word to go for direction for your specific need. You can also ask godly friends what Scripture passages have been meaningful and inspiring to them.

How will you live out Life Principle 3 this week? Discuss other ways that you can keep God's Word as your anchor during difficult times. Also, talk about ways that the Bible has encouraged you and kept your focus on God in the past. Then spend time in prayer asking God to draw you into intimate communion with Himself and to transform your life so that you can affect the world for the sake of His kingdom.

Life Lessons to Remember

🌢 *Consider God's promises your spiritual anchors* (see Heb. 6:18–20).

🌢 *God always keeps the promises that He makes* (see Josh. 21:45).

🌢 *Be willing to patiently wait for God to fulfill His promises* (see Hab. 2:2–3).

Life Principle 4

The awareness of God's presence energizes us for our work.

Deuteronomy 20:1

Life's Questions

Ecclesiastes 2:24 teaches, "There is nothing better for a man than to ... tell himself that his labor is good. This also I have seen that it is from the hand of God." This may be a challenging verse for you, especially if you don't have a very fulfilling profession. Maybe you're a caregiver to your children, spouse, or aging parents and you do an immense amount of work that is sometimes thankless and exhausting. Even if you really like your job, you may not always find it enjoyable. Every occupation brings difficulties and frustrations with it.

How do you feel about the work that you do? Is it your dream job or just something that you do to pay the bills? Whatever your situation may be, God expects you to do your best at whatever you do. Whether it's people, politics, or other kinds of problems that are causing you distress, you may wonder how you can stay motivated and honor God in your labors. Life Principle 4 gives you this encouragement: *The awareness of God's presence energizes us for our work.*

What the Bible Says

Read Deuteronomy 20:1–4. What kind of assignment did God guarantee that Israel would face (1)?

Why might the people of Israel be terrified and discouraged (1)?

What did God promise He would do for them (4)?

———————— ∞ ————————

The word *afraid* in the Old Testament also means to **stand in awe of, revere,** or **respect.** Only God deserves your awe, respect, and reverence (see Deut. 3:22). He is with you and He is able to overcome anything that you'll ever face.

———————— ∞ ————————

Read Deuteronomy 11:7–12 and review why God was giving these commands to Israel. Why was it important for the people of Israel to stay focused on God during this crucial time in the nation's history?

What It Means

The people of Israel were right: they could not conquer the Promised Land on their own. That's why it was imperative for them to look to God for courage and grace whenever they faced challenges, enemies, or seemingly impossible situations.

You may be wondering what this has to do with your particular job. As a believer, you're a servant of the living God every moment, with every task. Whether you're driving enemy armies out of the Promised Land, changing diapers, making multi-million dollar deals, delivering pizzas, or teaching a Sunday school class, you must honor God in all that you do.

Life Examples

What is the worst job that you can think of? Why is it so terrible?

Read Genesis 39:20–23. What do you imagine Joseph's life was like in the prison?

Why did the chief jailer have such confidence in Joseph (22–23)?

--- ∞ ---

*J*oseph spent at least a decade in that prison, but none of it was wasted time. God used that invaluable experience to teach him the principles that he would need when governing Egypt and to position him for maximum impact and blessings.

--- ∞ ---

Read Genesis 41:15–16, 38–44. How did God bless Joseph's faithfulness?

Living the Principle

How can you stay motivated and honor God in your work? Joseph did it by remembering that God was with him no matter what happened. He set his heart to serve God faithfully, whether in the prison or the palace and regardless of famine or fruitfulness. The same should be true for you. Colossians 3:23–24 instructs, "Whatever you do, do your work heartily, as for the Lord rather than for men, knowing that from the Lord you will receive the reward of the inheritance. It is the Lord Christ whom you serve."

Like Joseph, you may not know why God has allowed the difficulties that you face in your labors. It's possible that you have a certain goal in mind with regard to your profession, but God's plan for you is much greater. Obey Him and don't lose heart (see Gal. 6:9). Whether it's a battle with an enemy, an overwhelming challenge, or a personal crisis that appears impossible to overcome, God is with you. He is your energy, strength, wisdom, and creativity. He is also your boss. Do your very best for His sake and allow Him to work through you. He's got a great victory and a wonderful reward for you if you'll trust Him and do as He says.

——————— ∞ ———————

Lovingkindness is Yours, O Lord, for You recompense a man according to his work. (Ps. 62:12)

——————— ∞ ———————

How will you live out Life Principle 4 this week? Have you encountered a situation in your work that causes you fear or discourages you? Discuss ways that you can keep your mind focused on God's presence and honor Him in your work. Then spend time in prayer, asking God to draw you into intimate communion with Himself and to transform your life so that you can affect the world for the sake of His kingdom.

Life Lessons to Remember

🕯 *View yourself as a servant* (see Phil. 2:5–7).

🕯 *Realize that you work for the Lord Himself* (see Eph. 2:10).

🕯 *Realize that your pay comes both now and hereafter* (see 1 Cor. 3:13–14).

Life Principle 5

God does not require us to understand His will, just obey it, even if it seems unreasonable.

Joshua 3:8

Life's Questions

Are things not going the way you planned? Is it difficult for you to understand what went wrong in your situation or why God isn't blessing you? Sometimes it feels as if God is no longer working in your life because you've insisted on doing something your way instead of His way. Perhaps you've placed a condition on God: you only obey Him when you think His instructions are logical. What that really means is that you've failed to commit yourself to Him completely, and that's bound to cause frustration in your life.

Are you hesitant to obey God because He's commanded you to do something that you're not comfortable with or that you think is irrational? If your prayers seem unanswered and the path ahead appears blocked, then it could be that God is waiting for you to take the step of faith that He's commanded. Don't lose hope about your circumstances. Instead, embrace Life Principle 5: *God does not require us to understand His will, just obey it, even if it seems unreasonable.*

What the Bible Says

Read Joshua 3. What were the people to look for when crossing the Jordan River (3)?

Why would the people have been fearful about crossing the Jordan (4)?

——————— ∞ ———————

*T*he Jordan normally has many fording places, but this episode takes place during the grain harvest, when the spring rains and the melting snow from Mount Hermon would have flooded the Jordan's banks, making it completely impassable. Also, enemies and beasts such as vipers, scorpions, crocodiles, and panthers, could hide in the overgrown brush along the banks.

——————— ∞ ———————

What was God's promise to the people if they obeyed Him (5)?

What was God going to teach the Israelites (7–11)?

What do you think would have happened if the Israelites had not obeyed God?

What It Means

If you were planning to lead an enormous group of people across an overflowing river into enemy territory, probably the last thing you would do is send your most important people with your most valuable possession in first to test the waters, especially rushing flood waters. Yet, that is exactly what God sent Israel's priests to do at the Jordan River. God's command did not make sense to them, but He had another purpose in mind, which was to teach them to always keep their eyes on Him instead of their circumstances.

Life Examples

Read Joshua 6. What was God's command to the Israelites concerning Jericho (2–6)?

Does this make any sense to you as a military strategy?

According to Joshua 6:5, what was going to make the walls of Jericho fall?

--- ∞ ---

*A*rchaeological discoveries have shown that Jericho's outer wall would have been approximately 6 feet thick, and the inner wall 12 feet thick.

--- ∞ ---

What was similar about this event and the crossing of the Jordan (6)?

How closely did the people of Israel have to obey (10)?

What was the result of the Israelites' obedience and God's faithfulness (20, 27)?

Living the Principle

What has God called you to do? Do His instructions seem extreme or confusing? Has He challenged you to do something that you don't feel capable of? It is not your job to understand God's plan, but it *is* your responsibility to obey Him. God sees the beginning, middle, and end of your situation; therefore, His perspective about what He has called you to do is far more complete than yours. If you could just see things from His point of view, you would be highly motivated to obey Him.

--- ∞ ---

True obedience means doing what God says, when He says it, how He says it should be done, until what He says is accomplished—regardless of whether you understand the reasons for it or not.

--- ∞ ---

Unfortunately, if you disobey Him, you will continue to struggle in the same area repeatedly, and you will lose out on His blessings. God's goal is to grow your trust in Him, so He will give you assignments that test your heart and mature your faith. The good news is that, when you submit to God, He shows you His faithfulness and empowers you by His Holy Spirit to do everything that He calls you to do. Your obedience—even though you don't understand what He is doing—exercises your faith, making it stronger.

How will you live out Life Principle 5 this week? Discuss what appears "illogical" about what God has commanded you to do. Why does His direction intimidate you? How can you overcome your feelings of fear or confusion? Remember, your goal isn't to understand God's will; your goal is to step forward in obedience and faith. Therefore, encourage one another to do whatever God has called you to do. Then spend time in prayer asking God to draw you into intimate communion with Himself and to transform your life so that you can affect the world for the sake of His kingdom.

Life Lessons to Remember

❧ *Obedience must be the top priority of your life* (see Ps. 119:145).

❧ *The Holy Spirit enables you to walk obediently before God* (see John 14:26).

Life Principle 6

*You reap what you sow, more than you sow, and later than
you sow.*
Judges 2:1–4

Life's Questions

When you think of how farmers operate, Life Principle 6 makes perfect sense: *You reap what you sow, more than you sow, and later than you
sow.* If the farmer places tomato seeds in the ground, it's because he
wants to grow tomatoes. He will harvest the product of the kind of
seed that he has planted. The farmer takes from the ground far more
than he puts into it. The tiny seed reproduces itself many times over,
sprouting and becoming a plant that produces fruit, which will then
yield many more seeds. Of course, this is not an instantaneous process.
The farmer must wait for the crop to mature in its time. The rewards
of the harvest always come later than the initial investment.

What seeds are you planting? What would you like to accomplish with
your life? It's extremely important for you to be conscious of what you
are sowing with your words and actions because they set the direction
of your life.

What the Bible Says

Read Deuteronomy 7:1–6. What was God's command to Israel (1–2)?

Why was the Lord so strict about this issue (4)?

∞

$\int$dolatry in the Old Testament was often prompted by legit-imate needs. For example, **Baal** was the Canaanites' storm and fertility god who controlled the rain for the harvest. Instead of trusting God to provide for them, the Israelites turned to Baal, thinking that they'd have a better yield. They didn't have faith that God would provide for their needs, even after He had done so much for them. What do you turn to instead of God for *your* needs?

∞

What was the Lord's motivation in giving them this command (6)?

Read Judges 1:27–34. Why do you think the Israelites ignored God and failed to drive these foreign nations out?

Read Judges 2:1–4. What did the Israelites reap from their disobedience (3)?

What It Means

Did the Israelites allow the other nations to stay because they could profit from them? Was it because it was too much effort to drive them out? Whatever the case, they failed to honor God and their disobedience brought them a great deal of trouble. They weren't judged immediately, yet the consequences came all the same.

———————— ∞ ————————

It's a dangerous thing to think, **God won't mind.** He **does** mind when we disobey. You may not immediately see the consequences of your actions, but they are coming.

———————— ∞ ————————

Judges 2:10–11 reports, "All that generation also were gathered to their fathers; and there arose another generation after them who did not know the LORD, nor yet the work which He had done for Israel. Then the sons of Israel did evil in the sight of the LORD and served the Baals." Because of their disobedience, the Israelites suffered hundreds of years of warfare with the nations that they failed to drive out, as you can discover in Judges, 1 and 2 Samuel, 1 and 2 Kings, and 1 and 2 Chronicles.

Life Examples

Read Galatians 6:7–10. Why do you think Paul says, "God is not mocked" (7) about the things that you reap and sow?

What actions or attitudes do you consider "sowing in the flesh" (8)? What actions or attitudes do you consider "sowing in the Spirit"?

─────────── ∞ ───────────

*T*his principle is not about doing "good works." It's about being obedient to God. Plenty of people do "good works" with selfish intentions, and Jesus says to them, "I never knew you; DEPART FROM ME, YOU WHO PRACTICE LAWLESSNESS" (Matt. 7:23).

─────────── ∞ ───────────

Why do good deeds and obedience take more time and effort than doing evil (9)?

What will you reap if you obey God and don't lose heart?

Living the Principle

Do you seek God's leadership when you make a decision? Do you obey Him as soon as you know His will? Each choice that you make for good or evil is a seed which you are planting for your future, and sometimes it's the smallest decisions that affect you the most. This is because sin turns your heart away from God, while obedience turns your heart toward Him. If you fill your life with His Spirit and Word, you will reap the fruit of the Spirit (see Gal. 5:22–23) and enjoy all that you were created for. If you're disobedient, greedy, and selfish, then you're going to reap the terrible consequences of your ungodly lifestyle.

It's time to get serious about following God. You must decide what kind of life you are going to live and commit yourself to it because someday soon you'll see the return of what you've planted over the years. Will that be a crop that you're proud of?

How will you live out Life Principle 6 this week? Discuss what God is calling you to sow with your life. Is there any area of your life where you are already seeing a harvest? Then spend time in prayer, asking God to draw you into intimate communion with Himself and to transform your life so that you can affect the world for the sake of His kingdom.

Life Lessons to Remember

🌱 *God's commands apply to everyone, Christians and non-Christians* (see 2 Cor. 5:9–11).

🌱 *We reap what we sow* (see Luke 6:43–45).

🌱 *We reap more than we sow* (see John 12:23–25).

🌱 *We reap later than we sow* (see Isa. 49:4; Mark 9:41).

Life Principle 7

The dark moments of our life will last only so long as is necessary for God to accomplish His purpose in us.

1 Samuel 30:1–6

Life's Questions

Sometimes it seems as if the trials never really end—you're either beginning one, in the middle of one, or just ending a season of difficulties. Whether relational, financial, physical, or spiritual, these challenges can be very draining and discouraging. Also, problems don't happen in a vacuum—there are always new emergencies and troubles to deal with that make life even more difficult.

Yet God is *always* good. This may be a difficult truth to accept while you're going through a trial, but it's one that you need to cling to if you want to make it through. It's also helpful to remember Life Principle 7: *The dark moments of our life will last only so long as is necessary for God to accomplish His purpose in us.*

What the Bible Says

Read 1 Samuel 27:1–8. David had been anointed king of Israel by Samuel (see 1 Sam. 16:11–13) while the present king, Saul, was still alive. What is going on at this point in David's life (1)?

∾

---

*D*avid didn't have it easy. In addition to waiting years for God to give him the throne, King Saul wanted to kill him and anyone who helped him (see 1 Sam. 18:25; 19:10–12; 20:33; 22:17, 22; 23:8, 14–15, 24–25; 24:2; 26:2; 27:1).

∾

How long was David with the Philistines (7)?

Where did Achish the king of the Philistines tell David to dwell (6)?

What was wrong with this land (8)?

Read 1 Samuel 29:3–7. How did the Philistines react to having David in their midst (4)?

How do you think that David felt to be rejected in his homeland and by the Philistines?

Read 1 Samuel 30:1–6. What did David and his men find when they got home to Ziklag (1–3)?

Who did all the people blame for their misfortunes (6)?

What It Means

You can't blame David for despairing because everything was going wrong. He was unfairly targeted by King Saul, driven from his homeland, rejected by his new neighbors, and constantly under threat of attack. His family was taken captive, and his people were turning on him. If there were ever a moment for David to wonder what God was doing, this was it. Yet David did what we all should do when the dark moments of life overwhelm us. First Samuel 30:6 says, "David strengthened himself in the LORD his God." Instead of doubting God, David spent time in His presence, reminding himself of the mighty God that he trusted and served.

God chose David to be king of Israel years before David ever occupied the throne. God first had to prepare David to honor Him in everything that he did. There was **never** any question that God would keep His promise to David, no matter how David doubted or suffered. All of the trials merely strengthened David's faith for the challenges to come.

Life Examples

Read Isaiah 30:18–21. What does God want to do (18)?

When you cry out to God, how does He respond (19)?

Why does God allow adversity in your life (20–21)?

Living the Principle

Trials are confusing and are never easy. But God uses them to develop important character traits in your life, and you can profit from your troubles if you will trust Him. David did and he passed the tests of faith (see 1 Sam. 31:6; 2 Sam. 2:4; 5:1–5). God taught David through affliction, and He is teaching you as well.

———————— ∽ ————————

If you're walking with God and want to be used by Him, you will go through difficult times in your life.

———————— ∽ ————————

You may wonder, *Why does it have to be so painful?* Unfortunately, there are no simple answers because God's discipline and instruction are unique to each individual. God must get your attention, teach you to turn only to Him, and train you to minister to others who have profound hurts (see 2 Cor. 1:3–4)—and usually that requires touching an area deep within your soul. However, you can know for sure that He is doing something immensely important in and through you. God would never allow you to suffer without a significant reason or permit your trouble to continue a minute more than necessary. Therefore, don't run from your problems. Face them with faith in God, knowing that He will not give you more than you can bear.

How will you live out Life Principle 7 this week? Are you experiencing a dark, difficult time? Do you need the relief that only God can give? Discuss how to "strengthen yourself in the Lord" as David did and encourage each other. Then spend time in prayer, asking God to draw you into intimate communion with Himself and to transform your life so that you can affect the world for the sake of His kingdom.

Life Lessons to Remember

❦ *God has put a limit on all adversity* (see Lam. 3:31–33).

❦ *Adversity is God's tool for building godly character in us* (see Rom. 5:3–4).

❦ *Adversity usually comes in the areas where we feel the most confident* (see 2 Cor. 12:7–9).

❦ *God's ultimate design is to conform you to the likeness of Jesus* (see Rom. 8:29).

Life Principle 8

Fight all your battles on your knees and you win every time.
2 Samuel 15:31

Life's Questions

Have you ever been wrongly accused by someone you know? Have you ever endured the wrath and rejection of a co-worker or loved one? Perhaps some of the most hurtful situations that you've experienced came through the condemnation of a person that you cared about. Whether or not you merited their criticism, the pain which they inflicted was no doubt devastating and probably took a long time to overcome.

What can you do when you're betrayed and your heart is broken by another? How do you protect yourself from their ongoing attacks? As a child of God, you have a responsibility to respond in a godly manner when someone challenges you to combat, and Life Principle 8 holds the key to turning your circumstances around: *Fight all your battles on your knees and you win every time.*

What the Bible Says

Read 2 Samuel 13:1. Who were Absalom, Tamar, and Amnon?

Read 2 Samuel 13:6–14, 23–28. What did Absalom do to avenge his sister Tamar (28)?

Read 2 Samuel 13:37–38. What was Absalom forced to do?

These verses were given to you as background into Absalom's character. What is your initial impression of him?

Eventually, Absalom returned to Israel. Read 2 Samuel 15:1–12. Do Absalom's actions confirm your initial impression of him?

*H*ebron was where David was anointed king of Israel (see 2 Sam. 5), and it was also where Abraham, Isaac, and Jacob were buried. It was a symbolic center of Israel's leadership, making it the perfect place for Absalom to stage his coup. With the murder of David's firstborn son Amnon and the death of his second son Chileab (also called Daniel), Absalom was next in line for the throne and he was ready to take it.

Do you think that Absalom's time away from Jerusalem healed the anger that he had toward Amnon? Why or why not?

Read 2 Samuel 15:13–16, 23–31. How do you think David felt when he found out that his son had betrayed him?

What was David most interested in finding out (25–26)?

——————— ∞ ———————

*A*lmost 1,000 years after David went to the Mount of Olives to seek God, his descendant, Jesus the Messiah, went there, too. At the foot of the Mount of Olives is the garden of Gethsemane where Jesus accepted the Father's will (see Luke 22:42) and prepared to do battle with our sin on the cross.

——————— ∞ ———————

What did David finally ask of God (31)?

What It Means

Can you imagine how devastating it was for King David to be betrayed by his son? In every way, this was a lose-lose situation. David could not regain his kingdom without hurting his son and many of his countrymen, and he couldn't restore his relationship with his son while the kingdom hung in the balance. No slingshot or sword would solve his problem, but God could.

Life Examples

Read Psalm 3. When have you felt as David did in verses 1–2?

——————— ∞ ———————

*D*avid wrote Psalm 3 while he was fleeing from Absalom.

——————— ∞ ———————

Why was it important for David to know that the Lord was his shield during this time (3)?

What would you say David's mood was in the midst of this terrible trial (6–7)?

Are you encouraged by the fact that your vindication comes from God? Why or why not?

Living the Principle

God eventually delivered the kingdom of Israel back into David's hands and, although David did everything he could to protect him, Absalom still lost his life (see 2 Sam. 18). That is what always happens when a person harbors unforgiveness and revenge in his heart—he hurts the people around him unnecessarily and eventually destroys himself. That is why, whenever people attack you, you can't just react to them out of your fear and rage. You must be like David and have a battle plan. Your combat strategy must begin and end with getting on your knees and realizing that God is in control of your situation. He will handle everything for you if you will humble yourself and obey Him. However, you must stop being distracted by your own feelings and the details of your circumstances, and you must put your focus on Him and what He can teach you. Whenever you surrender yourself completely to God and trust Him with your struggles, you'll find that He is faithful to lead you to victory.

How will you live out Life Principle 8 this week? Are you facing a battle that seems like a lose-lose situation? Are you heartbroken by someone's accusations? Discuss your battle plan for taking your trouble to God and surrendering yourself to Him. Then spend time in prayer, asking God to draw you into intimate communion with Himself and to transform your life so that you can affect the world for the sake of His kingdom.

Life Lessons to Remember

❦ *Prayer and obedience to God are the biblical approaches to overcoming all of our troubles (see 2 Chron. 7:14; Phil. 4:6–7).*

❦ *You can remain firm in your faith only when you completely submit all areas of your life to God (see James 4:7–10).*

Life Principle 9

Trusting God means looking beyond what we can see to what God sees.

2 Kings 6:17

Life's Questions

You don't know what tomorrow may bring. This truth may cause you some anxiety, but when your faith is in God, it *should* bring you hope. God sees tomorrow—*all* of your tomorrows—and He is able to prepare you for whatever is to come. What is it about the future that causes you to be afraid? Is it a conflict that you dread? Are you doubtful about ever receiving your heart's desire? Are you caught in a bad situation that you fear will never change?

Your apprehension may come from viewing your circumstances through your own limited perspective. Instead, you should be confident that God is working on your behalf in ways that you cannot see. Life Principle 9 teaches: *Trusting God means looking beyond what we can see to what God sees.* The circumstances and obstacles that you observe today may be truly overwhelming, but God's resources are even greater and more powerful than you can imagine. God knows what is ahead and He is ready to deal with it. Therefore, put your faith in Him and obey whatever He says.

What the Bible Says

Read 2 Kings 6:8–23. How did Elisha know where the Arameans were going to ambush the Israelites (9–12)?

---------- ∽ ----------

The secret of the LORD is for those who fear Him. (Ps. 25:14)

---------- ∽ ----------

How did the king of Aram respond when he realized that Elisha had learned his secret plans (12–14)?

How would you have reacted if you were Elisha's servant (15)?

Do you think Elisha was surprised by the Aramean army? Why or why not?

Why do you think Elisha could see the Lord's forces, but the servant couldn't (16–17)?

The Aramean army started out hunting Elisha and ended up following him to Samaria. Why do you think they agreed to follow him (19–20)?

--- ∞ ---

$\mathcal{W}$e think of Jerusalem as the capital of Israel, but after Solomon's reign in 922 B.C., the nation was divided into two kingdoms: Israel and Judah. Jerusalem remained the capital of Judah, while Samaria became the capital of Israel. Elisha led the Aramean army 12 miles from Dothan into the heart of Israel.

--- ∞ ---

What It Means

To judge any situation by your limited perspective means that you aren't getting the whole picture. Elisha understood this, which is why he was so eager to hear whatever God had to say to him. He learned to look beyond what he could see to the Lord's reality, and God showed Elisha amazing things and did miracles through him.

Life Examples

Read 1 Corinthians 2:9–16. Why does Paul include eyes, ears, and hearts in verse 9? What does this suggest about God's perspective and your perspective?

According to verse 10, what is the only way that we can know what God is doing in our lives?

--------------- ∞ ---------------

Elisha's mentor, Elijah, was taken up to heaven, and Elisha asked him for a double portion of his spirit (see 2 Kings 2:9).

--------------- ∞ ---------------

Why does God communicate to us through the Spirit (11–13)?

What will worldly people think when they hear God's plans (14)? Why?

Why should God's plans make sense to you if you've accepted Christ as your Savior (15–16)?

Living the Principle

How did Elisha know the Arameans' plans and that the Lord's army was protecting him? He listened to the Spirit of God. You may think it is difficult to pay attention to God when you face overwhelming troubles, especially those that seem impossible. Like Elisha's servant, your mind searches for a way to deal with what you're seeing. In despair you cry out, "What can I do?"

∞

---

*C*all to Me and I will answer you, and I will tell you great and mighty things, which you do not know. (Jer. 33:3)

∞

The first thing that you must do is close your physical eyes because they're not helping. Stop measuring your problems against your own ability to handle them because the enemy will use your worldly senses to magnify what you're going through. Then you must open your spiritual eyes, the ones that are fixed upon God. Worship Him. Read His Word. Pray. Remember how He has helped others in the past, and thank Him that the mighty wisdom and power available to them has been provided to you, as well. God is ready, willing, and able to rescue you from the jaws of defeat, and He will do whatever is necessary to lead you to triumph when you obey Him.

How will you live out Life Principle 9 this week? Discuss how you will focus your mind and heart on God's truth rather than on what you can see. Then spend time in prayer, asking God to draw you into intimate communion with Himself and to transform your life so that you can affect the world for the sake of His kingdom.

Life Lessons to Remember

🌱 *Recall past victories* (see Ps. 145:5–7).

🌱 *Reject discouraging words* (see Ps. 40:14–16).

🌱 *Recognize the true nature of the battle* (see Ps. 20:6–8).

🌱 *Respond to the challenge with a positive confession* (see Ps. 118:6–9).

🌱 *Rely on the power of God* (see Ps. 66:3–5).

🌱 *Reckon the victory* (see Ps. 98:1).

Life Principle 10

If necessary, God will move heaven and earth to show us His will.

2 Chronicles 20:12

Life's Questions

What is God's will for your life? Do you have an answer, or do you think, *Good question! If He tells you what He wants me to do, please let me know.* Perhaps you know how God is leading you in certain areas of your life, and you're committed to following Him. However, there are other situations that you are facing in which you have no idea about what to do, and you wish that God would show you the right course of action. You wonder, *Why does God's will seem hidden from me? Can I truly know what God has planned for my life?*

Yes, you can! God does not hide His will from you. Rather, as Life Principle 10 states, *If necessary, God will move heaven and earth to show us His will.* So what is going on? Why is God's will such a mystery to you at this point?

What the Bible Says

Read 1 Kings 16:30–33. What kind of man was Ahab, the king of Israel?

―――――― ∞ ――――――

*A*hab was the seventh king of Israel. Through his wife, Jezebel, he brought the Phoenician religion to Israel. He set the deities of Tyre—Baal and Asherah—as equal with the Lord God and allowed Jezebel to kill the prophets and priests of God.

―――――― ∞ ――――――

Read 2 Chronicles 17:3–4 and 18:1–3. Considering his values, do you think it was wise for Jehoshaphat to ally himself with Ahab? Why do you think he did so?

Read 2 Chronicles 18:28–34. How did God show Jehoshaphat that an alliance with Ahab was *not* His will (31–34)?

Read 2 Chronicles 19:1–3. How did God confirm that Jehoshaphat had done the wrong thing?

What had Jehoshaphat done that was pleasing to God? What idols need to be removed in your own life?

What It Means

We do not know why Jehoshaphat decided to ally himself with Ahab. It could be that he saw an opportunity to reunite the kingdoms of Israel and Judah as they had been under David. It could also be that he thought an alliance with Israel would strengthen his military position or increase his wealth. Whatever the case, he failed to seek God and depend on Him for everything, and it nearly cost him his life.

Life Examples

Read 2 Chronicles 20:1–30. What terrible threat was Judah facing (1–2)? How did Jehoshaphat react?

What was God's message to Jehoshaphat (15)?

Why do you think God refused to allow Jehoshaphat to participate in the battle?

God's instruction to Jehoshaphat required a great test of faith. Do you think that Jehoshaphat learned his lesson about trusting God (18)?

What did Jehoshaphat instruct the people of Judah to do (20–21)?

When did God deliver the victory to Judah (22)? What is the connection?

Yet You are holy, O You who are enthroned upon the praises of Israel. In You our fathers trusted; they trusted and You delivered them. (Ps. 22:3–4)

Living the Principle

The battle is not yours, it belongs to God. What does this have to do with God's will? It means that God's will is *His* to communicate and fulfill. No matter what God reveals to be His plan, He will make sure that everything is in place for it to come to pass. Your responsibility is simply to obey Him *right now*. It is God's right to exclude or include you from the battle as He so desires.

God knows precisely what it will take to get your attention.

Perhaps the reason that God's will remains a mystery to you is that He is showing it to you one step at a time. Yes, God knows every detail of your circumstances and how they will all unfold, but He will not reveal them all at once. Instead, He will use this situation as an opportunity to teach you to trust Him. Unfortunately, if you are unwilling to wait for His timing and insist on having an answer about something specific, you are going to prolong your struggle and miss maturing in your faith.

Another reason you may think that God's will is hidden from you is that you've failed to obey Him in some area. God has shown you what to do, but His command seems unreasonable or un-important to you. Understand that you will not be able to move forward until you submit to Him in every area that He has called you to obey. Just like Jehoshaphat, you must surrender yourself to God com-pletely, whether it means engaging in the battle under God's leadership or watching what He is doing from the sidelines.

How will you live out Life Principle 10 this week? Are you having trouble discerning God's will? Discuss how God may be trying to get your at-tention, whether through your restless spirit, an unusual blessing, un-answered prayer, disappointment, financial trouble, or affliction. Then spend time in prayer, asking God to draw you into intimate communion with Himself and to transform your life so that you can affect the world for the sake of His kingdom.

Life Lessons to Remember

🌱 *God always knows exactly where we are in our journey of faith* (see Rom. 8:29–30).

🌱 *God is committed to helping us live out the specific plan that He has designed* (see Jer. 29:11–13).

Life Principle 11

God assumes full responsibility for our needs when we obey Him.

Job 42:7–17

Life's Questions

It's in times of great loss or trial that you may be tempted to question whether God really cares about you. After all, certain things have gone terribly wrong and you find that there are needs in your life that continue to go unmet. You believe that He is God—fully able to provide for you—so the questions arise, *Why isn't God delivering me from all of this? Why has He allowed these bad things to happen to me? Haven't I been faithful? Does He really want to help me?*

Yes, He does. In fact, God takes great joy in meeting your needs and supplying the desires of your heart. Yet there is a condition. Life Principle 11 explains, *God assumes full responsibility for our needs when we obey Him.* Are you submitting yourself fully to God? Are you trusting Him despite your circumstances?

What the Bible Says

Read Job 1:1–3 and 6–12. What was Satan implying about why Job served God (10–11)?

Why do you think God allowed Satan to test Job (8, 12)?

Read Job 1:13–22. What do you think about Job's response to his adversity (20–21)?

Read Job 2:1–10. Why do you think Job was able to remain so strong in the midst of such terrible pain and loss (10)?

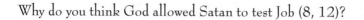

The LORD *gave, and the* LORD *has taken away; blessed be the name of the* LORD. (Job 1:21)

What would you have done if you had been in Job's shoes? Do you think your faith would have withstood all of those trials?

Read Job 42:1–17. According to verse 5, what need did God fill for Job that was not fulfilled by all the things that he'd lost?

∞

Though He slay me, I will hope in Him. (Job 13:15)

∞

Why did Job need to lose so much before he could come to this profound understanding of God?

Why do you think God gave *twice* as much as Job had before (10, 12)?

What It Means

Job obeyed God, but bad things still happened to him—overnight he found himself in deep pain and terrible need. Why? Was it merely to prove something to Satan, or was there a deeper reason? God was meeting more important needs in Job than we may initially realize. Remember Life Principle 1: *Our intimacy with God—His highest priority for our lives—determines the impact of our lives.* God took full responsibility for bringing Job into the deepest intimacy possible with Himself. And because of Job's obedience, people throughout the ages have been encouraged by his faithful example.

——————— ∞ ———————

He knows the way I take; when He has tried me, I shall come forth as gold. My foot has held fast to His path; I have kept His way and not turned aside. (Job 23:10–11)

——————— ∞ ———————

Life Examples

Read Luke 11:9–13. What is God's promise to you (9–10)? What can you expect from God (11–12)?

Why can you count on God to give His very best for you (13)?

Living the Principle

There are two questions that you must settle in your heart: First, *can* God help you? Do you believe that God is completely *able* to intervene in your situation? Do you have confidence in the One who laid the foundations of the earth (see Gen. 1), who delivered the children of Israel out of Egypt and parted the Red Sea (see Ex. 14:13–31), and who defeated death to save you from your sins and provide a home for you in heaven (see 1 Cor. 15)?

The second question is: *will* God help you? Romans 8:32 answers that question for you. "He who did not spare His own Son, but delivered Him over for us all, how will He not also with Him freely give us all things?"

God is both able and willing to supply *everything* that you need. Therefore, if there are still areas in your life where you are lacking, spend time in prayer asking God to reveal what He is trying to teach you. Maybe there is something in your life that shouldn't be there, or perhaps He is filling a deeper need in you as He did with Job.

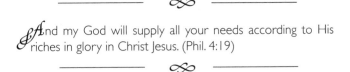

And my God will supply all your needs according to His riches in glory in Christ Jesus. (Phil. 4:19)

How will you live out Life Principle 11 this week? Is there something that you are in need of? Is God trying to reveal something special to you? Discuss ways that you can stay faithful to God as Job did, even when you don't understand what is going on. Then spend time in prayer, asking God to draw you into intimate communion with Himself and to transform your life so that you can affect the world for the sake of His kingdom.

Life Lessons to Remember

🌱 *God is able to provide for us* (see Ps. 65:4–6).

🌱 *God's integrity and love ensure that He will carry out His promises to us* (see Ps. 37:25–28).

Life Principle 12

Peace with God is the fruit of oneness with God.
Psalm 4:8

Life's Questions

At night when everything is quiet, uneasy thoughts can bombard you. You want to sleep and get the rest that you need, but your responsibilities and problems fill your mind. You try to focus on other things—counting sheep or the tick-tocks of your clock—but you can't stop the anxieties from tormenting you and keeping you awake. In those moments, you would give anything for some peace.

Have you experienced sleepless nights alone with your troubled thoughts? Have you struggled through those stressful moments, wondering why your mind cannot let go and rest? You know that in John 14:27, Jesus said, "My peace I give to you; not as the world gives do I give to you. Do not let your heart be troubled, nor let it be fearful." But why is that peace so hard to hold on to? Peace is God's gift to you, but you cannot have it apart from a close, intimate relationship with Him. As Life Principle 12 states, *Peace with God is the fruit of oneness with God.*

What the Bible Says

Read 2 Samuel 19:9–15 and 40–43. Why were the people of Israel protesting?

—————— ∞ ——————

*W*hen the Israelites spoke of their "ten parts in the king" (2 Sam. 19:43), they were referring to ten tribes. There were 12 tribes of Israel in total, but the tribe of Simeon was within the borders of Judah (see Josh. 19:1) and was considered part of Judah.

—————— ∞ ——————

Read 2 Samuel 20:1–7. How widespread was Sheba's rebellion (2)?

How serious did David consider this rebellion to be (6)?

Read 2 Samuel 20:15–22. How did God turn Sheba's rebellion around to restore the peace of Israel?

Read Psalm 4. Why was it important for David to remember that God had relieved him of his distress in the past (1, 3)?

———————— ∞ ————————

S'ome believe that Psalm 4 was written either during the rebellion of Sheba or while Saul was persecuting David. Others believe that Psalm 4, like Psalm 3, was written by David during Absalom's rebellion against him. No matter who sought to hurt him, David trusted in God for his peace.

———————— ∞ ————————

Why did David write verses 4–5? Why would this be important to remember in times of great stress and conflict?

What can you learn about David's relationship with God from verses 7–8?

Why did David's relationship with God give him peace?

———————— ∞ ————————

The word *peace* in Hebrew, *shalom,* means *the completion, fulfillment, unity, and harmony that come as a result of God's presence*.

———————— ∞ ————————

What It Means

Considering that David had so many enemies, it is difficult to imagine him getting a good night's sleep. However, David knew that he could rely upon God for his safety and peace. This was the result of his faithful walk with the Lord. David was committed to obeying God and keeping his focus continually on Him. Because of that, David had peace, even in the worst situations.

Life Examples

Read Isaiah 26:3–4. When have you spent an extended period in prayer and worship, meditating on God's Word and enjoying His presence?

Did your time with God fill you with peace? Why or why not?

Why would keeping your focus on God fill you with peace?

Living the Principle

Do you long for deep, abiding peace? Does your soul need rest from the worries and stresses that surround you? Your anxiety is a telltale sign that your focus isn't where it should be. Instead of rejoicing in the strength, wisdom, and love of God, you've allowed your attention to be consumed by the details of your circumstances. You are so busy trying to figure out how to fix your situation that you've forgotten that the only effective solution is to submit yourself to God. As Jesus said, "I have spoken to you, so that in Me you may have peace. In the world you have tribulation, but take courage; I have overcome the world" (John 16:33).

Therefore, you must learn to think differently, or as Romans 12:2 instructs, "Be transformed by the renewing of your mind." The most important thing is to begin every day by reading God's Word and spending time in prayer. Your time with God will give you the direction, strength, and focus that you need and will fill you with the assurance that your heart yearns for.

———————— ∞ ————————

The word **peace** in Greek, **eirene**, means **to bind together**. It is the harmony, security, and joy that come from a relationship with Jesus Christ.

———————— ∞ ————————

How will you live out Life Principle 12 this week? Discuss the trials that you are facing and how you can develop your "oneness" with Christ. Then spend time in prayer, asking God to draw you into intimate communion with Himself and to transform your life so that you can affect the world for the sake of His kingdom.

Life Lessons to Remember

❦ *Only God is equipped to handle our problems* (see Ps. 62:5–7).

❦ *Accepting God's timetable and instruction helps to dispel rising anxiety* (see Hab. 2:1–3).

❦ *The safest place for you when trials come is in the everlasting arms of Jesus* (see Deut. 33:27).

Life Principle 13

Listening to God is essential to walking with God.
Psalm 81:8

Life's Questions

Have you ever been in a situation where people simply didn't listen to you, even though you knew exactly what you were talking about? The solution to the problem seemed obvious to you, but others were so busy voicing their opinions that you couldn't get a word in edgewise. Frustrating, wasn't it? Now imagine what it must be like to be God in heaven, with the most profound and complete knowledge about every topic in the universe. He has the wisdom that we need to solve all of our problems, even the deepest ones. Unfortunately, whenever we bow our heads in prayer to communicate with Him, we do all the talking.

Is that what you do? Have you been one-sided in your conversations with God, telling Him your needs instead of listening to His instruction? Life Principle 13 states, *Listening to God is essential to walking with God.* You can't have a relationship with someone that you don't listen to. If you want God to lead you and transform your life, then you need to hear what He's saying.

What the Bible Says

Read Psalm 81. Why was it important for the Israelites to recall all the good things that God had done for them on the full moon, Sabbath, and other feast days (1–7; see also Deut. 4:7–10)?

———————— ∞ ————————

The full moon marked the beginning of the month, in which the Israelites would give offerings to God. It was a celebration of how He had worked among them (see Num. 10:10; 28:11–15).

———————— ∞ ————————

How does recalling God's past provision help you when you pray?

What did God want from Israel (8–10, 13–16)?

In what ways was God being gracious in His commands?

How did Israel respond to God (11–12)?

Why do you think Israel refused to listen to Him? Do you fail to listen to Him for similar reasons?

What It Means

God wants the very best for those who believe in Him, and He knows exactly how to provide it. Unfortunately, the people of Israel did not trust Him enough to embrace what He was teaching them, and time after time they experienced the terrible consequences of their disobedience. They refused to listen to God, thinking that by doing so they were escaping His control. However, what they were really doing was rejecting His protection and love. Don't make the same mistake. God's commands are for your benefit. As Proverbs 1:7, 33 says, "The fear of the LORD is the beginning of knowledge ... he who listens to me shall live securely and will be at ease from the dread of evil."

Life Examples

Do you do all the talking in your relationship with God? Why or why not?

Read Ecclesiastes 5:1–3. What attitude should you have when you go to God in prayer?

What do many words in prayer actually reveal? Why do you think this is?

Charles Stanley

———————— ∞ ————————

A true conversation involves both talking and listening.

———————— ∞ ————————

Read Matthew 6:5–8. What does Jesus mean when He says that the hypocrites have their reward (5)?

Why is your prayer to be in secret, but God's reward is out in the open (6)?

What does Jesus say about the use of many words (7)?

If God already "knows what you need before you ask Him" (8), then why should you go before Him in prayer?

Living the Principle

Do you realize the amazing privilege that you have in being able to go to God in prayer? You have the freedom to approach the God of all creation at any moment to ask for His wisdom, comfort, and power. Hebrews 4:15–16 affirms, "We do not have a high priest who cannot sympathize with our weaknesses, but One who has been tempted in all things as we are, yet without sin. Therefore let us draw near with confidence to the throne of grace, so that we may receive mercy and find grace to help in time of need."

Jesus understands everything that you're going through and all that you feel, and His desire is to guide you through your troubles in a way that glorifies God and makes you into an effective, mature believer. However, He cannot help you if you will not walk with Him, and you cannot walk with Him if you won't allow Him to lead you. And unfortunately, He cannot lead you if you refuse to listen to Him.

How will you live out Life Principle 13 this week? Are you willing to be quiet before Him and hear what He has to say? Create an action plan of how you will intentionally listen to God and commit yourself to obeying Him, no matter what He tells you to do. Also, discuss how you will keep each other accountable regarding those plans. Then spend time in prayer, asking God to draw you into intimate communion with Himself and to transform your life so that you can affect the world for the sake of His kingdom.

Life Lessons to Remember

* *God is not silent* (see Heb. 1:1–3).

* *God always speaks for your benefit* (see Isa. 51:1–16).

Life Principle 14

God acts on behalf of those who wait for Him.
Isaiah 64:4

Life's Questions

Waiting is not fun. Each day you wake up hoping for some tidbit of good news, but it doesn't come or you receive a negative report, and you see longer delays ahead. It can be very frustrating. No wonder Proverbs 13:12 tells us, "Hope deferred makes the heart sick." The longer you wait to see your desire fulfilled, the more discouraged your heart grows. That is, of course, unless your hope and trust are centered exclusively on Christ.

One of the most difficult lessons that you will learn is to wait on God. However, it is crucial that you understand how truly important waiting on Him is. Life Principle 14 explains, *God acts on behalf of those who wait for Him.* If you want God's very best for your life, you must trust Him to provide it *in His time.* His knowledge of you and your situation are absolutely perfect—and so is His timing. He is going to make sure that you are completely prepared for the blessings that He has for you. Therefore, make sure to keep your eyes on Him.

∞

Isaiah ministered to Judah from 740 BC to 681 BC, and he prophesied about the Babylonian captivity which would begin a century later in 597 BC. The Babylonians would also destroy the temple in Jerusalem (see Isa. 63:18) in 586 BC. In Isaiah 63:7–64:12, the prophet thanks God for His mercy in delivering the church from the Babylonian captivity.

∞

What the Bible Says

Read Isaiah 63:7–14. How does Isaiah describe God (7–9)?

How did the people respond to God's kindness (10)?

Why does God discipline His people (10; see also Heb. 12:5–11)?

What did the people do after God disciplined them (11–13)?

Read Isaiah 63:15–19. How did the people of Judah feel as they were held captive in Babylon? When have you felt this way?

Read Isaiah 64:1–4. What did Isaiah ask God to do (1–3)?

What other hope was there for the people (4)?

What It Means

It is true that God was preparing His judgment for the kingdom of Judah, but He was also arranging the deliverance of the people who remained obedient to Him. Their only hope was to wait on God to rescue them from their captors. Thankfully, it was a sure hope, and God was faithful to bring them back to Jerusalem when the time was right and their hearts had turned back to Him (see Ezra and Nehemiah). As God promises in Isaiah 49:23, "You will know that I am the LORD; those who hopefully wait for Me will not be put to shame."

Life Examples

Read Isaiah 40:27–31. What are you waiting for? Do you ever feel that your situation is "hidden from the LORD" (27)?

What does God do for you as you wait (29)?

————————— ∞ —————————

*W*hen you wait for the Lord, you should look forward to what He will do with joyful expectation and confident hope, because He is providing His very best for you.

————————— ∞ —————————

God understands how difficult the delays are for you (30). How does this encourage you?

What promise does God make to you if you commit yourself to waiting for Him (31)?

Living the Principle

During your season of waiting, you may feel somewhat lost, discouraged, and unmotivated. You may also feel as if God has forgotten you. He has not. God is always at work, and at this very moment He is engineering your situation to provide His very best for you. In fact, He is lining up your circumstances in a way that is better than you could ever imagine (see Eph. 3:20–21), and you are going to be completely blessed when you see what He has done for you.

However, you must be patient until His plan comes together in His perfect timing. Do not run ahead of God! The delays may be very challenging for you, but they are growing your faith in Him. After all, "Faith is the assurance of things hoped for, the conviction of things not seen" (Heb. 11:1). Therefore, look to Him, strengthen yourself in His Word and love, and remain confident that He is working on your behalf.

Of course, you may be wondering, *What does God want me to do during this waiting time? Am I just supposed to sit around and do nothing?* Absolutely not! Waiting on God simply means that you continue in your present position until He gives you further instructions. As long as you are obeying Him, you will continue on the correct course.

How will you live out Life Principle 14 this week? Discuss times that you've waited for God to work and describe how He acted on your behalf. Then spend time in prayer, asking God to draw you into intimate communion with Himself and to transform your life so that you can affect the world for the sake of His kingdom.

Life Lessons to Remember

🌸 *When we wait, we discover God's will in the areas that most concern us* (see Isa. 30:18).

🌸 *When we wait, we receive supernatural physical energy and strength* (see Ps. 27:13–14).

🌸 *When we wait, we win battles* (see Ps. 59:9–10).

🌸 *When we wait, we see the fulfillment of our faith* (see Ps. 33:20–21).

🌸 *When we wait, we see God working on our behalf* (see Ps. 40:1–3).

Life Principle 15

Brokenness is God's requirement for maximum usefulness.
Jeremiah 15:19

Life's Questions

Sometimes it just doesn't make sense. You seek God and try to be obedient to Him, but trouble and heartbreak confront you at every turn. Perhaps you thought that life would get easier after you accepted Christ as your Savior, but you've found just the opposite to be true. Now you have to deal with the troubles that the world throws at you, and you also feel responsible to honor God in how you respond to them. Somewhere inside of you, you've come to the realization that you're just not strong enough to live the holy life that Christ has called you to.

Good! God never meant you to live the Christian life by your own resources. The trials that you've been experiencing are part of the breaking process, whereby God frees you from your self-sufficiency so that you'll allow Christ to live in and through you. That's why Life Principle 15 teaches, *Brokenness is God's requirement for maximum usefulness.* It's through brokenness that you stop depending on yourself and start looking to Him for your strength, wisdom, and power.

What the Bible Says

Read 2 Kings 21:1–16. How did Manasseh's sin affect Judah (9–12, 16)?

Read Jeremiah 15:4–6. What was God's judgment upon Judah?

——————— ∞ ———————

*J*eremiah was a prophet in Judah from 627 BC to c. 586 BC. He served *after* Manasseh's reign (c. 685 BC to 630 BC), but the ongoing corruption of the king's idolatry was felt throughout Judah for many years (see Ex. 20:4–5; Jer. 15:4). God's punishment for Judah was the Babylonian captivity. Jeremiah's sad duty was to warn the people of the judgment that was coming.

——————— ∞ ———————

Read Jeremiah 15:15–21. How did Jeremiah respond to God's verdict (15)?

What was Jeremiah's concern about God's judgment (18)? When have you ever felt as Jeremiah did?

What was God's promise to Jeremiah (19–21)?

What do you think it means to "extract the precious from the worthless" (19)?

——————— ∞ ———————

*N*othing could prevent God's judgment, yet Jeremiah was still responsible to proclaim the truth to those who were perishing, in the hope that they would repent and be saved (see Jer. 18:8).

——————— ∞ ———————

How do you think God would make Jeremiah into "a fortified wall of bronze" (20; see also Jer. 1:18–19)?

What It Means

At times, the suffering that you go through will seem immensely un-fair, especially when it occurs at the hand of another person. Jeremiah was a godly man who had to endure the consequences of Manasseh's sin, even though he had nothing to do with the king's wickedness. Still, God used the pressure to make Jeremiah into His holy mouthpiece, and Jeremiah's words have endured throughout the generations, bring-ing hope to countless people undergoing similar persecution.

You must remember that, even when the adversity that you are experi-encing appears to be senseless, "God causes all things to work together for good to those who love God, to those who are called according to His purpose" (Rom. 8:28). That trial has been allowed in your life for an eternal reason—a purpose beyond what you can see or understand at the moment. However, you can be absolutely confident that God will use it for good in your life if you submit yourself to Him and trust Him (see 1 Peter 2:19–20).

Life Examples

Read 2 Corinthians 1:3–11. How does Paul describe God in verse 3?

How does God treat you while you are going through adversity (4)?

What is God training you to do as He is comforting you (4–5)?

What did Paul see as the purpose for his great suffering (8–10)?

Living the Principle

Romans 8:20–21 explains, "The creation was subjected to futility, not willingly, but because of Him who subjected it, in hope that the creation itself also will be set free from its slavery to corruption into the freedom of the glory of the children of God." In other words, you've experienced these frustrating trials so that you can be free of the sin nature that is left within you. Yes, you are forgiven of *all* your sin when you accept Christ as your Lord and Savior. However, the tendency to *want* to sin remains within you, and He must break you of it.

God does so for two reasons: to transform you into the image of Christ (see Rom. 8:29; Eph 5:1) and to develop your potential as His representative in the world (see Phil. 3:9–10; Col. 1:24; Heb 2:18; 1 Peter 4:12–16). Therefore, commit yourself to God and heed the words of 1 Peter 4:19: "Those also who suffer according to the will of God shall entrust their souls to a faithful Creator in doing what is right."

——————— ∞ ———————

*F*or it was fitting for Him, for whom are all things, and through whom are all things, in bringing many sons to glory, to perfect the author of their salvation through sufferings. (Heb. 2:10)

——————— ∞ ———————

How will you live out Life Principle 15 this week? Discuss the trials that you are facing and encourage each other to remain faithful and obedient to God. Then spend time in prayer, asking God to draw you into intimate communion with Himself and to transform your life so that you can affect the world for the sake of His kingdom.

Life Lessons to Remember

🌱 *Through brokenness, you gain a new perspective of God's mercy and provision* (see Ps. 73:25–26).

🌱 *You develop a more complete comprehension of yourself* (see Ps. 73:21–23).

🌱 *Your compassion and understanding for the suffering of others grows* (see Heb. 5:2).

Life Principle 16

Whatever you acquire outside of God's will eventually turns to ashes.

Ezekiel 25:6–7

Life's Questions

The temptation sits before you, beckoning you to come take it. It looks so much like the desire of your heart that you can't stop thinking about it. An alarm goes off within your spirit: something just isn't right about what you want to do. Still, the opportunity is so enticing that you shake off the warning, thinking, *Why not? God doesn't really care about this, does He?* You know that He does, so the argument in your mind continues, *What if this is my only chance to be happy? God wouldn't deny me that, would He? What if God never gives me what I really want?*

When thoughts like that enter your mind, remember Life Principle 16: *Whatever you acquire outside of God's will eventually turns to ashes.* You are about to enter dangerous territory that will disappoint you, and may destroy you, as well.

———— ∞ ————

For hundreds of years, the Ammonites conspired to run the people of God out of the Promised Land (see Judg. 3:10–12; 2 Sam. 10; 1 Chron. 19–20; 27:5; Ps. 83:3–8). So when God rebuked Judah for its sin, He simply took His hand of protection off of His people and allowed the Ammonites to attack. Still, God is just. He faithfully judged Ammon for its sinfulness (see Jer. 49:1–6; Ezek. 21:28–32; 25:1–7; Amos 1:13–15).

———— ∞ ————

What the Bible Says

Read Zephaniah 2:8. What was Ammon's intention regarding the people of God?

Read Ezekiel 21:28–32. The Ammonites found an ally in the Babylonians. How did God warn the Ammonites against helping them?

How did the Babylonians convince the Ammonites to help them (29)?

Read 2 Kings 24:1–4. Did Ammon heed God's warning? Why not, do you think?

Read Ezekiel 25:1–7. What was particularly distressing about the Ammonites' attitudes as they plundered Judah (3, 6)?

What was God's response to the Ammonites (4–7)?

What It Means

The Ammonites were descendants of Lot, Abraham's nephew (see Gen. 12:5; 19:36–38), so they were both neighbors of Judah and Israel and related to them as well. The Ammonites could have learned to honor God and enjoy His blessings (see Deut. 2:19). Unfortunately, they were more interested in possessing the land of their relatives than in knowing their God, and because of it they came to a bitter end: no land, no God, no nation—nothing. Everything that they had turned to ashes, even though God gave them ample time to repent. Don't make their mistake.

——————— ∞ ———————

Babylonian King Nebuchadnezzar betrayed Ammon, attacking its capital city around 581 BC. Ammon never recovered, and eventually the nation died out completely. During the third century BC, Ptolemy II Philadelphus renamed the city Philadelphia. It received its current name—Amman, Jordan—in the third century AD.

——————— ∞ ———————

Life Examples

Read 1 Corinthians 3:9–15. When you became a Christian, what role did you take on (8–11; see also Eph. 2:19–22)?

What must you constantly have in mind as you go about your day (11)?

80

What different motivations are there for doing work (12–13; see also 4:5)?

What type of work will endure (14)? What will be burned up?

Read 1 Peter 1:13–21. What is Peter's challenge to you?

Living the Principle

What do you long for? Is it love, wealth, acceptance, stability, prominence, or something else? If you chase after it apart from God's will, what you'll find once you achieve your goal will be extremely disappointing and empty. It will burn up and turn to ashes, and it will singe you in the process, as well. Therefore, don't ignore the alarm signal within you—it is God's Holy Spirit warning you that you're about to do something that you will regret.

Rather, trust God and be holy as He is holy (see 1 Peter 1:15–16). Resist the temptation to go after the desire of your heart in your own strength and by your own means, remembering that God will provide the absolute best for you if you will trust and obey Him. Those blessings will endure, and they will be to God's glory in eternity. As David wrote, "You will make known to me the path of life; in Your presence is fullness of joy; in Your right hand there are pleasures forever" (Ps. 16:11).

———————— ∞ ————————

Delight yourself in the LORD; and He will give you the desires of your heart. (Ps. 37:4)

———————— ∞ ————————

How will you live out Life Principle 16 this week? Do you believe that God's will is truly best for you? Why or why not? Discuss ways to make sure that you are seeking God's will and ways to resist temptation when it beckons to you. Then spend time in prayer, asking God to draw you into intimate communion with Himself and to transform your life so that you can affect the world for the sake of His kingdom.

Life Lessons to Remember

🌱 *When we pursue our desire in opposition to God's will, we end up truly disappointed* (see Ps. 106:15).

🌱 *As we pursue God, He fulfills the other desires that He has given us* (see Ps. 37:5).

Life Principle 17

$\mathscr{W}$e stand tallest and strongest on our knees.
Daniel 6:10–11

Life's Questions

Following God isn't easy. The world that persecuted the prophets and crucified Christ often responds negatively to those who are committed to the Lord (see Matt. 5:10–12). Jesus explains the reason: "If they persecuted Me, they will also persecute you.... All these things they will do to you for My name's sake, because they do not know the One who sent Me. If I had not come and spoken to them, they would not have sin, but now they have no excuse for their sin" (John 15:20–22). When others see God working through you, they will be convicted of their sin, which will make them very uncomfortable. This means that they may lash out at you or try to undermine your testimony.

Have you encountered trouble because you're a Christian? Have you found it difficult to get along with particular people or in certain situations because you follow God? Then discover the way that the saints before you defended themselves. Life Principle 17 teaches, *We stand tallest and strongest on our knees.*

$\mathscr{D}$aniel was of royal birth but was taken captive to Babylon as a young man. He was an impressive individual and was quickly recruited to serve in the king's palace (see Dan. 1:3–4), where he was careful to continue honoring and obeying God in every way. He ministered throughout the Babylonian captivity and shortly thereafter (c. 605 BC to 530 BC).

What the Bible Says

Read Daniel 6:1–9. How did Daniel distinguish himself and how did the king reward him for it (3)?

Why do you think the commissioners and satraps wanted to get rid of Daniel?

What plot did they invent to trap him (4–8)?

Read Daniel 6:10–17. Why did Daniel disobey the decree (10)?

In view of the plot against him, why wasn't Daniel more secretive about praying to God?

How did the king react to Daniel's violation of the decree (14, 16)?

Read Daniel 6:18–28. How did God honor Daniel's faithfulness (22)?

What ultimately came from Daniel's obedience to God (26–28)?

What It Means

The strength of Daniel's character came from his time alone with God; he remained steadfast because he was consistent in praying to God and obeying His commands. His eyes were not

on his foes or on the ravenous lions. He did not worry about pandering to the commissioners and satraps or trying to gain political points with the king. Rather, Daniel's complete attention was on God. He knew that he could not go wrong as long as he was honoring God because his Lord would defend him.

Life Examples

Read 1 Peter 5:6–11. What is God's promise to you if you obey Him (6)?

What "lion" do you have to watch out for when you submit yourself to God (8)?

From Daniel's example and verse 9, what have you learned about fighting the enemy? What will result from your obedience (10–11)?

--- ∞ ---

What will your submission to God do? It will **perfect** you, which means to restore, mend, render complete, and equip. It will **confirm** you, which means to make as solid as granite, make stable, place firmly, and render constant. It will **strengthen** you, which means to make strong or fill with strength. And it will **establish** you, which means to lay the foundation of your faith and your future with Christ.

--- ∞ ---

Living the Principle

Being on your knees before God isn't just a physical stance. It's an attitude of the heart in which you are seeking God and are willing to submit to His plan for your future. As you spend time with Him in prayer, your relationship with God becomes deeper and more intimate. You feel His power in your life and begin to trust His hand in every situation. Instead of worrying about the "lions" in your path, you increasingly focus on Him and how He is working. This gives you the assurance and boldness to face your troubles, because you're confident that God's plan for you will be accomplished.

Prayer is the most powerful thing that you can do. As difficult conflicts arise, the enemy may try to convince you to "tone down" or keep your walk with God a secret. However, God will call you to a deeper walk with Him so that you can experience His provision, grow in your faith, and be a shining example to others.

How will you live out Life Principle 17 this week? You stand tallest and strongest on your knees because that is when you submit yourself to God. Will you commit yourself to Him in prayer? Discuss ways that you can deepen your time alone with the Lord. Then spend time in prayer, asking God to draw you into intimate communion with Himself and to transform your life so that you can affect the world for the sake of His kingdom.

Life Lessons to Remember

🍇 *God is greater than any problem that we could ever face* (see 1 John 4:4).

🍇 *Whatever we face, we must trust God with it* (see 2 Sam. 22:2–4).

Life Principle 18

As children of a sovereign God, we are never victims of our circumstances.

As children of a sovereign God, we are never victims of our circumstances.

Hosea 3:4–5

Life's Questions

There are tragic, life-changing moments that can be extremely difficult to survive. An unexpected trial strikes you with a force that knocks you off your feet, the pain and loss far more intense than you ever thought possible. Stunned and overwhelmed, your mind will look for some explanation to cling to. You may wonder, *What did I do to deserve this? Why would God allow this to happen to me?* During these times of heartbreak, it is extremely important for you to remember Life Principle 18: *As children of a sovereign God, we are never victims of our circumstances.* You may not know why this adversity has come into your life, but you can trust that God is with you and loves you.

What the Bible Says

Read Hosea 1:1–3. What did the Lord command Hosea to do?

———— ∞ ————

Hosea was a prophet in the northern kingdom of Israel c. 755 BC to 715 BC. God brought His judgment to the kingdom of Judah through Babylon, and He judged Israel through the Assyrian invasion.

———— ∞ ————

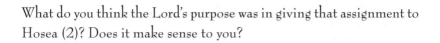

What do you think the Lord's purpose was in giving that assignment to Hosea (2)? Does it make sense to you?

Read Hosea 2:6–8, 13. What did Israel do?

What was God's judgment concerning Israel's unfaithfulness? What was Israel supposed to learn from God's rebuke (7–8)?

——————— ∞ ———————

*T*he Hebrew word for *master* or *owner* is ***Baal****.* The Lord is your true Master and Owner. However, you always need to be careful that your full affection is set on Him so that something else—such as wealth, relationships, power, or status— doesn't control you and become your god.

——————— ∞ ———————

Read Hosea 2:14–20. What would God do *after* He judged Israel's sin?

What is the difference between thinking of God as your *Husband (Ishi)* and thinking of Him as your *Master (Baali)* (16)? Isn't He both?

What do verses 19–20 tell you about God's intentions toward you?

———————— ∞ ————————

Hosea loved and cared for Gomer, yet she went back to prostitution and was enslaved to another man. Hosea was then forced to purchase her for half the price of a female slave (see Ex. 21:32).

———————— ∞ ————————

Read Hosea 3:1–5. How was God's relationship with Israel reflected in Hosea's relationship with Gomer?

What do you think the Israelites learned from not having kings, princes, and so on (4)?

What is God's goal for every circumstance that comes into your life (5)?

What It Means

Through Hosea's marriage, God gave the Israelites the perfect picture of what He wanted to teach them. They had sinned, abandoning the God who redeemed them from Egypt to run after false deities that couldn't offer them anything but heartache. Still, God loved His people, and He was committed to the covenant that He had made with them. He was willing to take drastic measures—even allowing Assyria to invade them—to bring Israel back to a vibrant relationship with Himself. In fact, Hosea 3:5 says, "Afterward the sons of Israel will return and seek the LORD their God and David their king." This meant that they would embrace the descendant of David who would become their Messiah. Through this conflict with Assyria, God would prepare the people of Israel for Jesus to be their Savior.

Life Examples

Read Psalm 103:19. What does God rule over? Is there anything in all creation that God does not control?

How does this apply to the trial that you are experiencing?

Living the Principle

God is completely sovereign, which means that everything that touches your life must serve some purpose. Nothing that happens to you is ever meaningless or useless. You are never merely a victim of an unfair world. God has a very important purpose for refining you, which is to conform you to the image of His Son and glorify Himself through you. The more jolting the hardship, the greater the ministry which God is preparing for you. The deeper the cut, the more profoundly God will use you to do His work in the world if you will trust and obey Him.

Are you in the middle of a trial? Do you wonder why God has allowed such a painful experience in your life? It is all right to ask Him why He permitted the adversity and what He wants you to learn from it. However, you must avoid becoming bitter and resentful. Always remember that God is ultimately in control, His love for you never changes, and His will for your life is good. You are not a victim. You are God's beloved child and He has an extraordinary plan for your life, so have faith in Him.

How will you live out Life Principle 18 this week? Discuss how it helps you to know that God has a purpose in all of your circumstances. Then spend time in prayer, asking God to draw you into intimate communion with Himself and to transform your life so that you can affect the world for the sake of His kingdom.

Life Lessons to Remember

❦ *Your sovereign God has determined to use everything that happens to you for your blessing and His glory* (see Rom. 8:28).

❦ *To endure, keep your eyes on Jesus* (see Heb. 12:1–3).

Life Principle 19

Anything you hold too tightly, you will lose.
Amos 6:6–7

Life's Questions

What can you not live without? What would utterly devastate you if you lost it? Is it a relationship, possession, or a certain situation in your life? Is it more important to you than God? You need to consider how tight a hold it actually has on you because it could become counter-productive and even dangerous. What would you do if God asked you to give it up? Could you obey Him? Does the thought of letting it go cause you to feel anxious and out of control?

If there is something in your life that could keep you from trusting and honoring the Lord, it is an idol, and God is not going to allow you to keep it in your grasp. Life Principle 19 teaches, *Anything you hold too tightly, you will lose.* If you are looking to anything other than God for your sense of acceptance, accomplishment, and security, then you are headed for serious trouble, because it will not last. Sooner or later, God will assert His rightful role as the only Lord of your life.

--- ∞ ---

Amos was a shepherd and farmer in Judah who warned Israel about God's coming judgment (c. 760 BC to 750 BC). King Jeroboam II had expanded Israel's territory and wealth, but the prosperity corrupted the people and they became even more immoral and idolatrous.

--- ∞ ---

What the Bible Says

Read Amos 2:6–8. How were the Israelites displeasing to the Lord?

Read Amos 6:1–8. What were the Israelites trusting in (1)?

What attitude were the people of Israel exhibiting in verses 4–5?

What do you think the "ruin of Joseph" was (6; see also Ezek. 34:2–4)?

What did God hate about Israel's behavior (8; see also Ps. 10:2–4)? What was God's punishment (7)?

What It Means

The Israelites were so enamored with their prosperity that they forgot God (see Hos. 10:1–3). They became prideful in their affluence and military victories and believed that they didn't need Him anymore. So when God called them to repentance, they refused to obey His commands or let Him back into their lives. They just weren't willing give up their wealth and ease for Him—and it cost them everything.

Life Examples

Read 2 Kings 17:5–20. How did Amos' prophecy come true (5–6)?

How had God warned them (13)? How does He use similar methods today to warn people about their sinfulness?

How did the Israelites respond to God (14–17)?

What happened to everything that the Israelites were trying to hold onto (18–20)?

Israel's capital, Samaria, was destroyed in 722 BC by Assyria. Thousands of Israelites were taken captive to Media and Upper Mesopotamia. The rest were made to live under Assyrian rule, and Israel itself ceased to exist. From there, the land changed hands many times, and Israel did not become a nation again until May 14, 1948.

Living the Principle

God sent prophets to Israel and Judah before sending His judgment (see Amos 3:7). As we discussed in Life Principle 10, *God will move heaven and earth to show you His will*. God wants you to know what is going on and what His plan is for you. However, no matter what the circumstances may be, your most important responsibility is always to trust and obey Him. If there is something that you are honoring above

God, He will let you know that it displeases Him and He will call you to lay that person, possession, or situation down on your own. However, if you refuse to submit it to Him, He will pry it out of your hands, which is always extremely painful.

God will not share the control of your life with something or someone else. Jesus said, "No one can serve two masters; for either he will hate the one and love the other, or he will be devoted to one and despise the other" (Matt. 6:24). You neither honor God nor help yourself by having a divided heart. Therefore, make a decision about what will rule your life once and for all. Surrender whatever is coming between you and the Lord.

The good news is that, no matter what God requires you to give up, you can be certain that your life is going to be much better without it in the long run. God is not punishing you by taking this precious thing from you—He is preparing to give you something even better.

Keep your eyes on God and not the blessing.

How will you live out Life Principle 19 this week? Discuss what you are having trouble giving up and how you will keep each other accountable in honoring God. Then spend time in prayer, asking God to draw you into intimate communion with Himself and to transform your life so that you can affect the world for the sake of His kingdom.

Life Lessons to Remember

🌱 *God loves you too much to allow any notions of self-sufficiency or dependence upon anything other than Himself (see 2 Cor. 12:7–10).*

Life Principle 20

Disappointments are inevitable; discouragement is a choice.
Habakkuk 3:17–19

Life's Questions

Life often doesn't turn out the way that you think it should. Opportunities that you were counting on don't turn out the way that you thought they would. People that you thought you could depend on end up letting you down. Even the plans and expectations that you designed for yourself have been frustrated. It's all very disappointing.

What hopes do you have for your life? What opportunities, relationships, or situations are you constantly reaching for? It is human nature to have hopes—they motivate you and keep you striving for the best. Unfortunately, your expectations can also disappoint you terribly if they don't come true. During those times of disillusionment, the most important thing for you to remember is Life Principle 20: *Disappointments are inevitable; discouragement is a choice.* Will you allow your disappointments to dishearten you? Will you allow them to impede you from becoming everything that God created you to be? It's your decision, so choose wisely.

∞

The prophet Habakkuk ministered in Judah c. 612 BC to 588 BC, before and during the Babylonian invasion.

∞

What the Bible Says

Read Zephaniah 1:2–6. What was happening in Judah before the Babylonians invaded?

Read Habakkuk 1:1–6. What was Habakkuk's reaction to the idolatry, immorality, and injustice that he saw daily in his nation? What was God's response to Habakkuk (5–6)?

Read Habakkuk 2:2–4. Why does God tell Habakkuk to write down His judgment concerning Babylon (2–3)?

What is God's admonition to Habakkuk in verse 4?

Read Habakkuk 3:17–19. How does Habakkuk respond to God?

∞

The people of Judah were serving **fertility** gods—the basis for their idolatry was to increase their crops and prosperity. Habakkuk names all of the major crops of the region and says that, even if they all fail, God is still worthy of praise. That is the true heart of faith.

∞

What It Means

Life can be downright depressing at times. Habakkuk pleaded for God to rebuke the wickedness of his countrymen, but he became disheartened when he found out that the judgment would come in the form of Babylon's invasion of Judah. This is the very core of disappointment—you expect something that will improve your circumstances, but you receive something that makes your situation worse.

Habakkuk didn't understand God's ways, but he still trusted in God's wisdom. "I will exult in the LORD, I will rejoice in the God of my salvation. The Lord GOD is my strength" (Hab. 3:18–19). This is what you must do as well, even when God's answer to your prayers isn't what you were hoping for. Trust Him, because He knows exactly what He is doing.

Life Examples

Read Psalm 73:1–12. When have you doubted God because you saw someone else prospering in a manner that you've longed for?

Read Psalm 73:13–17. Have you ever been tempted to give up out of discouragement? If so, what brought you back into fellowship with God?

Read Psalm 73:21–28. As a believer, what do you have to rely on when all else fails? How can remembering this keep you from becoming discouraged?

Living the Principle

How do you respond when disappointments come your way? Do you become angry, frustrated, and disheartened? Or do you say, "Lord, I may not know why You allowed this, but I trust You anyway, knowing that Your best for my life is still ahead." If you respond with discouragement and resentment, you will begin a downhill slide away from God's purpose for your life. However, if you respond with trust and praise, it will build your faith and bring you closer to the Lord.

Whenever you face disappointments, remember that your situation is in His hand and under His sovereign control. Meditate on the fact that He loves you unconditionally and is providing His very best for you. Recall the blessings that He has already given you. No matter what disappointments come into your life, you can use them as stepping-stones to greater faith. Instead of becoming discouraged, you'll be filled with His courage, and there's nothing more encouraging than that.

The LORD is the one who goes ahead of you; He will be with you. He will not fail you or forsake you. Do not fear or be dismayed. (Deut. 31:8)

How will you live out Life Principle 20 this week? Discuss the disappointments that you've experienced recently and how you can turn them to your advantage by trusting God. Then spend time in prayer, asking God to draw you into intimate communion with Himself and to transform your life so that you can affect the world for the sake of His kingdom.

Life Lessons to Remember

❦ *God has a unique plan for your life that is not changed by unexpected circumstances* (see Isa. 41:9–10).

❦ *Whenever a situation arises that does not line up with your understanding of God's will, you must stop and look to Him for direction* (see Ps. 32:8).

❦ *God holds your future in His hands, and you will never lose by looking forward to what He has in store* (see Phil. 3:13–14).

Life Principle 21

Obedience always brings blessing.

Luke 11:28

Life's Questions

How far does God expect you to go in your obedience to Him? Perhaps you've accepted Jesus as your Lord and Savior and have submitted to Him in some important areas, but you're still not certain that you want to turn *every* part of your life over to Him. After all, as Paul wrote, "All things are lawful for me" (1 Cor. 6:12). Salvation is through faith in Christ and you can't lose it, so why do you need to obey His truly difficult commands?

Don't miss the rest of Paul's message. He writes, "All things are lawful for me, but I will not be mastered by anything.... You have been bought with a price: therefore glorify God in your body" (1 Cor. 6:12, 20). God wants you to enjoy the freedom which He gives you in every area (see Gal. 5:1, 13; James 1:25), but the only way to attain that liberty is through obedience. That's why Life Principle 21 teaches, *Obedience always brings blessing.*

People questioned the power by which Jesus cast out demons, and He replied, "If I cast out demons by the finger of God, then the kingdom of God has come upon you" (Luke 11:20). Jesus provides the only way that a person can be free, but He requires our obedience in the process.

What the Bible Says

Read Luke 11:23–28. What does Jesus mean when He says, "He who is not with Me is against Me; and he who does not gather with Me, scatters" (23)?

Why can people turn to religions, rehabilitation programs, psychotherapy, etc., and *appear* to get better, only to relapse into their old ways after a while (24–25)?

What do those belief systems and programs actually make room for (26)? What does this say about how Satan influences people's lives?

Can a person be *possessed* by a demon once Jesus Christ becomes their Savior and Lord (see 1 Cor. 3:16; 6:17; 1 John 4:4)?

In what ways can you be *influenced* by the enemy (see 1 Cor. 10:13; Eph. 4:27; James 1:14)?

∞

As a "new creature" in Christ (2 Cor. 5:17), only the Holy Spirit can dwell in you (see 1 Cor. 6:19–20). The enemy's unclean spirits no longer have a place in you.

∞

What does Jesus admonish you to do (see Luke 11:28)?

What It Means

The enemy wants to control and destroy you (see 2 Thes. 1:8–9). That is why Satan will do whatever he can to keep a person from realizing his need for salvation through Jesus Christ. Once you receive Jesus as your Savior and His Holy Spirit comes to live in you, you can no longer be possessed by the enemy's demons or be forced to do his will (see Eph. 4:30; 2 Tim. 2:26). The only thing that the enemy can do is destroy your effectiveness for the kingdom of God and stop you from enjoying the relationship that you have with God. The enemy does this by tempting you to sin.

Therefore, whenever you *disobey* God, you are actually participating in the enemy's plot to injure you and make you miserable. You are also acting *against* Christ, rather than *with* Him. Christ calls you to obedience so that you may enjoy the abundant life that He created you for (see John 10:10). This is why He gives us His Spirit, "so that [you] may know the things freely given to [you] by God" (1 Cor. 2:12).

Life Examples

Read John 15:4–8. How do you produce something that is worthy and eternal (4–5)?

What is Christ's promise to you if you obey Him faithfully (7; see also Ps. 37:4)?

——————— ∞ ———————

The word *abide* in the New Testament means *to remain steadfast, persevering in being united as one with Christ in heart, soul, mind, strength, and will.* How do you remain so close to God? He'll show you as you do what He says.

——————— ∞ ———————

You exist to glorify God (see Ps. 86:8–12; Matt. 5:16); therefore, how do you best live out the purpose for which you were created (John 15:8)?

What kind of *fruit* is Jesus talking about (see Gal. 5:22–23; 1 Peter 1:5–8)? Do you exhibit these characteristics?

Read John 15:9–16. Why does Jesus have you join Him in doing His work in the world (11)?

What should your motivation be in everything that you do for God (9–10, 13–14)?

Why is it important to remember that you serve *with* God out of *friendship*, rather than *for* God out of *obligation* (15–16)?

Living the Principle

As your Creator and Owner, God knows what is absolutely best for you, and He wants to see it accomplished in your life. What is hindering you from obeying God? Are you holding on to a person, goal, or activity that is less than God's best for you? It may be frightening to submit it to God, but do it anyway. God wants to bless you and give you freedom in that area, but He will only do so when you obey Him. Is obedience sometimes challenging? Yes. But will it be worth it when you see God working in your life and experience His freedom? Absolutely! Therefore, obey God with confidence, knowing that you will be blessed when you do.

How will you live out Life Principle 21 this week? Discuss the areas of obedience that you are having trouble with and commit to keeping each other accountable in turning those areas over to God. Then spend time in prayer, asking God to draw you into intimate communion with Himself and to transform your life so that you can affect the world for the sake of His kingdom.

Life Lessons to Remember

🌸 *Obeying God in small matters is an essential step to God's greatest blessings* (see Mark 4:30–32).

🌸 *Our obedience always benefits others* (see 2 Cor. 4:11–15).

🌸 *When we obey God, we will never be disappointed* (see Ps. 22:5).

Life Principle 22

To walk in the Spirit is to obey the initial promptings of the Spirit.

Acts 10:19

Life's Questions

Do you ever feel burned out in your walk with God? Do you wonder if you are on the right track or if there is something more that you should be experiencing? Do you wish that God's direction were clearer to you? Then you may be trying to live the Christian life in your own strength and wisdom, rather than by following the leadership of God's Holy Spirit. Life Principle 22 teaches, *To walk in the Spirit is to obey the initial promptings of the Spirit.* When you do so, you are equipped and empowered by the Holy Spirit and have His perfect direction and guidance. The Holy Spirit may lead you in ways that you don't expect but as you obey Him, you see that He always directs you in the most blessed and effective path.

What the Bible Says

Read Acts 10:1–8. What sort of man was Cornelius (1–4)?

—————— ∞ ——————

*Cornelius was known as a **God-fearer**. This meant that he ascribed to Jewish worship and morals and believed in the One True God, but he probably wasn't a Jewish convert in the formal sense of being circumcised and undergoing Jewish baptism.*

—————— ∞ ——————

How specific was the Lord in His instruction to Cornelius (5–6)?

Why do you think Cornelius was so moved by this vision (7–8)?

Read Acts 10:9–16. How was Peter's response different than Cornelius's (14)?

Why do you think Peter answered the way he did (14; also see Lev. 11:4, 8)? What was God's answer to Peter (15)?

Why do you think this vision was repeated three times (16)?

Read Acts 10:17–23. How quickly did the Spirit reveal to Peter what the vision meant?

Read Acts 10:24–48. What opportunity did Peter receive because both he and Cornelius obeyed the Holy Spirit (33)?

How did Peter show that he had learned what God was teaching him through the vision (28, 34–35)?

———————— ∞ ————————

*F*or I am not ashamed of the gospel, for it is the power of God for salvation to everyone who believes, to the Jew first and also to the Greek. (Rom. 1:16)

———————— ∞ ————————

How were the people blessed by the obedience of Peter and Cornelius (44–45; also see 11:15–18)?

What It Means

Cornelius and the others were the first Gentile believers to become part of the church without first becoming Jewish converts. Before this, it was thought that Gentile believers could not receive the Holy Spirit because He was only given for the people of Israel. In other words, non-Jews were not considered full, complete Christians. Of course, this was not God's plan. Rather, it was based on the fact that only Jewish believers had received the Holy Spirit at Pentecost (see Acts 2:2–3). But when the Holy Spirit fell upon all those who heard the word (see Acts 10:44), just as He had at Pentecost, all of the Jewish believers there understood that God was extending His great gift to the Gentiles, as well.

Thankfully, neither Peter nor Cornelius ignored the promptings of the Holy Spirit because of their preconceived notions. Instead, because of their obedience, the way was opened for Gentiles to receive the Holy Spirit and become part of the Body of Christ. Unless you have a Jewish background, you are directly affected by this event. You do not have to go through all of the rituals and convert to Judaism before you can accept Christ as your Savior and receive the Holy Spirit. And we know this because these two men were obedient to the promptings of the Spirit.

Life Examples

Read Acts 16:6–10. How did the Holy Spirit direct Paul and Silas (6–7)?

Why did the Holy Spirit *prevent* them from preaching the gospel?

When has the Holy Spirit shut a door to you that you did not understand?

How did the Holy Spirit redirect Paul and Silas (9–10)?

——————— ∞ ———————

This was Paul's second missionary journey. He may have been looking forward to visiting the churches that he'd previously planted, but God had other plans—including crossing the Aegean Sea to a new continent (Europe) with the gospel. Paul subsequently planted churches at Philippi, Thessalonica, and Berea.

——————— ∞ ———————

Living the Principle

Have you been ignoring the Spirit's promptings because you are unsure about where He is directing you? Has the Spirit challenged your beliefs or is He moving you to change your course? The Holy Spirit can never lead you wrong because He guides you in doing God's will: which is glorifying God and becoming everything that He created you to be. Jesus said, "The Spirit ... will guide you into all the truth ... He will glorify Me, for He will take of Mine and will disclose it to you" (John 16:13–14).

The Holy Spirit is your Counselor, Comforter, and Helper, and He makes sure that you have everything you need to accomplish whatever God has called you to do. Therefore, you need to stop trying to do everything by your own power. Obey what the Holy Spirit is guiding you to do right away, and then watch and enjoy the wonderful Spirit-filled life that unfolds before you.

How will you live out Life Principle 22 this week? Discuss the challenges and blessings that come with obeying the initial promptings of the Holy Spirit. Then spend time in prayer, asking God to draw you into intimate communion with Himself and to transform your life so that you can affect the world for the sake of His kingdom.

Life Lessons to Remember

🌱 *We must stay yielded to the Holy Spirit* (see Rom. 8:13–14; Gal. 5:16–18).

🌱 *We must trust the Holy Spirit to guide us* (see 1 Thes. 5:19).

Life Principle 23

𝒴ou can never out give God.

2 Corinthians 9:8

Life's Questions

Giving is an aspect of discipleship that pastors are generally hesitant to talk about and believers are usually less than enthusiastic to learn. For some reason, the topics of tithing and generosity strike us as too personal to discuss and are often difficult to turn over to God. We're eager to receive God's blessings, yet we're hesitant to obey Him with the gifts that He's given us. This is due to a lack of trust and the refusal to acknowledge God's ownership of all that exists.

That's why Life Principle 23 teaches, *You can never out give God.* God is loving and full of grace, so when He commands us to let go of our wealth and resources, it is for a good reason. He does not want to deprive us. Rather, He wants to teach us to be more like Him by making us into generous givers. As we learn to let go of our possessions, we find that we receive back from Him above and beyond all we've released.

What the Bible Says

Read Acts 11:27–30. Why did the disciples find it necessary to send aid to the believers in Judea, and more specifically, the church in Jerusalem (28)?

Read 2 Corinthians 8:1–7. What example had the Macedonian churches set for the Corinthians (1–4)?

——————— ⨪⨪ ———————

*G*od sent Paul to the Macedonians during his second missionary journey, and this letter to the Corinthians was written during his third missionary journey a few years later. Paul couldn't have known what an immense blessing the Macedonian churches would be to him and to the church in Jerusalem, but God did.

——————— ⨪⨪ ———————

Why do you think Paul begins his plea to the Corinthians with the positive example of the Macedonians (7)?

Read 2 Corinthians 8:8–15. Why is it often easier to show your love and support for others in ways that are not financial (8)?

How did Jesus become poor for your sake (9; also see Phil. 2:5–7)?

When have you pledged to donate resources and then failed to make good on your promise (10–12)? What happened?

——————— ∞ ———————

*T*he Corinthians had pledged to give to the church in Jerusalem but had not yet fulfilled their promise.

——————— ∞ ———————

Why is it in your interest to be faithful to God with your finances (see Mal. 3:10) and to show generosity toward others (13–15; also see Luke 6:38; Gal. 5:13–15)?

What It Means

Along with the famine (see Acts 11:27–30), there were other factors affecting the poor in Jerusalem. Many believers were disowned by their families and community, losing their ability to support themselves. This led to the pooling of resources which were soon spent (see Acts 2:44; 4:34). There were also many widows that needed to be supported (see Acts 6:1–6), as well as missionaries that were being sent out. To make matters even worse, the people were being taxed by both Jewish and Roman authorities, which meant that it was nearly impossible to produce enough to live on. However, through all these financial troubles, God was teaching the Gentile believers to show His love to others, and He was also showing Jewish believers that they could trust the Gentile Christians. In other words, God was uniting the church that was divided by culture and distance as only He could.

Life Examples

Read 2 Corinthians 9:1–15. What do you think Paul told the Macedonians about the Corinthians (2)?

When people think of you as a good example, does it motivate you to act in a godly manner, even if it's difficult (3–5)? Why or why not?

How have you seen the principle in verse 6 proven true in your own life?

What is cheerful giving based on (7; also see Matt. 10:8; John 13:34; 1 Cor. 13:3; Eph 5:2)?

What is God's promise to you when you give (8)?

---------------- ∞ ----------------

The word **grace** in the New Testament comes from the root word **to rejoice.** It means **the absolutely free benefit or expression of loving-kindness, deeds which cause joy,** and **favor conferred.** When Paul writes, "God is able to make all grace abound to you" (2 Cor. 9:8), it means that God shows you a superabundance of kindness that will cause you immense joy.

---------------- ∞ ----------------

What does obedience to God in your finances inspire (10–15)?

Living the Principle

Do you tithe, giving ten percent of your income for the ministry of the church? Do you give generously, blessing those in need? Perhaps you look at those questions and think, *I can't because I have barely enough to live on myself.* Or maybe your response is, *I've worked hard for what I have and I don't see why I should give it up.* As we've discussed before, both of these attitudes come from a lack of trust in God and the refusal to acknowledge His ownership of all that exists. God wants to "open ... the windows of heaven and pour out for you a blessing until it overflows" (Mal. 3:10), but He will wait until you submit this area of your life to Him.

God knows your struggles, desires, and the circumstances that surround your life, and He has promised to "supply all your needs according to His riches in glory in Christ Jesus" (Phil. 4:19). So stop making your decisions based on a balance sheet, and start obeying God in every area, including your finances. You'll never come up short. Be generous with Him, and what you'll find are greater blessings than you could have imagined.

How will you live out Life Principle 23 this week? Discuss the blessings of turning your finances over to God. Submit to Him and commit to keeping each other accountable in the area of finances. Then spend time in prayer, asking God to draw you into intimate communion with Himself and to transform your life so that you can affect the world for the sake of His kingdom.

Life Lessons to Remember

* *All that we have is a gift from God; therefore, whatever we offer Him is only a portion of what He has already given to us* (see Deut. 10:14).

* *When we obey Him by honoring Him with our tithes, He protects our finances and blesses us* (see Mal. 3:10).

Life Principle 24

To live the Christian life is to allow Jesus to live His life in and through us.

Galatians 2:20

Life's Questions

What troubles your heart today? What concern is consuming you with fear and doubt? Do you realize that it's not your place to worry about that person, situation, or issue? Have you come to the understanding that everything that concerns you is Christ's responsibility to care for rather than yours and that your job is simply to obey Him? David wrote in Psalm 138:7–8, "Though I walk in the midst of trouble ... Your right hand will save me. The LORD will accomplish what concerns me."

You may be so used to taking care of yourself or others that this is a difficult truth to accept. However, if you will embrace Life Principle 24—*To live the Christian life is to allow Jesus to live His life in and through us*—then you will experience all of the peace, joy, confidence, and assurance that are rightfully yours in Jesus Christ. If you don't, then you'll continue being distracted by issues that were never yours to worry about, and you will miss the blessings of the abundant life that God planned for you.

The Jerusalem Council (see Acts 15) addressed the concerns of the Judaizers, who trusted Jesus as their Savior, but also believed that Christians should keep the law in order to attain salvation. Christ made no such requirement for salvation.

What the Bible Says

Read Acts 15:1–5 and Galatians 2:11–13. Why did Paul criticize Peter? What was the dispute?

Read Galatians 2:14–21. What is Paul's counsel to Peter, whom he calls Cephas in this passage (14)?

How is a person justified or saved (16; also see Acts 15:7–11)?

--- ∞ ---

*W*hen Peter spoke of the salvation of the Gentiles, he was referring to what had occurred as he was preaching to Cornelius and his household (see Acts 10).

--- ∞ ---

Why do you think our tendency is to be distracted by the law, good deeds, and religious activities (17–19)?

What is the true proof that you are saved (20)?

What does it mean to allow Christ to live through you? Is there anything specific that you should be doing (20; also see Rom. 6:5–13)?

Is allowing Christ to live through you easier or more difficult than following a set of rules? Why?

When you go back to living by the law or religious rituals instead of by God's grace, what are you really saying (21)?

What It Means

The Judaizers probably believed that they were guarding the faith. However, what they were really doing was being distracted by issues that weren't important and creating conflict within the church. Peter rebuked them by saying, "Why do you put God to the test by placing upon the neck of the disciples a yoke which neither our fathers nor we have been able to bear? But we believe that we are saved through the grace of the Lord Jesus" (Acts 15:10–11). What is distracting you from following God? What is creating a yoke of bondage on you that shouldn't be there? Are you worried that you're not doing enough to deserve a relationship with God? Are you concerned by some other issue and failing to trust God's sovereign hand in it? Then you need to return to the basic truth that your salvation is through faith in Christ, and your whole life must be as well.

Life Examples

Read Matthew 16:24–27. What does it mean to take up your cross (24)?

How do you lose your life for Christ's sake (25)? What life is it that you find (25–26)?

Why is it important that you guard your soul?

What promise do you have if you allow Christ to live through you (27)?

Living the Principle

God does not call you to an *adequate* life. He wants your life to be *extraordinary*. However, for you to experience the life that He planned for you, you must stop being distracted by peripheral issues and focus your attention completely on Him. Can you trust Jesus to live His life through you and take care of all that troubles you?

Of course you can! The God who saved you can teach you how to live for Him. The Lord who forgave your sins and gives you a home in heaven can surely attend to that person or situation that is causing you so much concern. And the Savior that you trusted for your eternity is more than capable of taking care of all the matters that burden you daily. Therefore, die to your worries so you can experience true life in Him.

———————— ∞ ————————

Let us run with endurance the race that is set before us, fixing our eyes on Jesus, the author and perfecter of faith. (Heb. 12:1–2)

———————— ∞ ————————

How will you live out Life Principle 24 this week? Discuss the distractions that have been troubling you and submit them to God. Then spend time in prayer, asking God to draw you into intimate communion with Himself and to transform your life so that you can affect the world for the sake of His kingdom.

Life Lessons to Remember

❧ *God desires an intimate, daily relationship with you in which you experience His presence, trust His wisdom, and rely on His strength* (see Isa. 58:2).

❧ *The Spirit-filled life is marked by purpose, power, and effectiveness* (see Rom. 8:14–17).

Life Principle 25

God blesses us so that we might bless others.
Ephesians 4:28

Life's Questions

Does your love for God motivate you to serve others? Does your relationship with Him inspire you to comfort other people just as He has done for you? This is the heart of Life Principle 25 and a truth which you must embrace if you want to experience the abundant life: *God blesses us so that we might bless others.*

You may feel that you don't have much to offer people, but you do. In fact, there are many ways that you can minister to others with the abilities and resources that God has given to you. If you know Jesus Christ as your Lord and Savior, you can share your faith with those who have never experienced forgiveness for their sin and don't know where they will spend eternity. If God has given you talents or provided you with a good income, you can help others with what you've been given. First Peter 4:10 teaches, "As each one has received a special gift, employ it in serving one another as good stewards of the manifold grace of God." Are you willing to be a good steward of what God has provided? Then look for opportunities to bless others.

What the Bible Says

Read Ephesians 4:1–6. What are the qualities of a life that is worthy of Christ (1–3; also see Col. 3:12–13)?

Why are these qualities important as you follow Jesus (4–6; 5:1–2)?

———— ∞ ————

$\mathcal{J}$esus poured out His life so that others could be saved (see Luke 19:10). If you're going to represent Him (see 2 Cor. 5:20), shouldn't you be like Him in character and purpose?

———— ∞ ————

Read Ephesians 4:7–16. What did Christ give believers so that they could bless one another (7–8)?

What is your spiritual gift (11–12; also see Rom. 12:4–8)? Why has that gift been given to you (13–16)?

Read Ephesians 4:17–32. What change is there to be in the way you view yourself and others (21–24; also see Phil. 2:1–4)?

What is to be your goal concerning others (28–29)?

Why do negative attitudes or selfish actions towards others grieve the Holy Spirit (30–31; also see Rom. 8:26–29)? What would bring joy to the Holy Spirit (32)?

What It Means

The Ephesian church was very blessed because Ephesus was a wealthy and influential city in Asia Minor which had extraordinary potential for spreading Christianity. As Paul sat in prison (see Eph. 3:1; 4:1; 6:20), he must have thought about the amazing influence for Christ that the Ephesians could have on the world. However, he knew that they first had to learn that their true wealth wasn't in earthly riches but in spiritual blessings by which they encouraged others (see Eph. 1).

Paul taught them in Acts 20:35, "In everything I showed you that by working hard in this manner you must help the weak and remember the words of the Lord Jesus, that He Himself said, 'It is more blessed to give than to receive.'" They needed to realize that the reason God had given them such immense blessings was so that they would use them for His glory and for the furtherance of the gospel. The same is true for you. God's gifts to you were never meant to be hoarded. They were given to be used wisely as you minister to others through the power and wisdom of the Holy Spirit.

———————— ∞ ————————

*Y*our Father has chosen gladly to give you the kingdom. Sell your possessions and give to charity; make yourselves money belts which do not wear out, an unfailing treasure in heaven, where no thief comes near nor moth destroys. For where your treasure is, there your heart will be also. (Luke 12:32–34)

———————— ∞ ————————

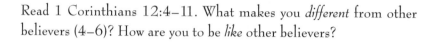

Read 1 Corinthians 12:4–11. What makes you *different* from other believers (4–6)? How are you to be *like* other believers?

For whom does the Holy Spirit give you gifts, talents, and blessings (7)?

Why do you think the Holy Spirit wanted you personally to have the gifts that you've received (11)?

Are you using your gifts in a way that honors God and blesses others?

Living the Principle

Who are the special people that God used to shape your life? Do you ever consider how much they gave for you and how willingly they shared the gifts that God provided to them? They were faithful to bless you with what God had given them, and you should be, too.

Can you be trusted with the blessings God has given you? Does your love for God motivate you to minister to others in His name and for His glory? Does your relationship with Him inspire you to give freely so others can know His salvation, comfort, and joy? Only you can stop God's goodness from flowing through your life and into the lives of others, and you do it by hoarding His gifts. Therefore, count your blessings and look for opportunities to shine His light and love into other's lives. Soon you'll see that it truly is much more blessed to give than to receive.

--- ∞ ---

If I am being poured out as a drink offering upon the sacrifice and service of your faith, I rejoice and share my joy with you all. (Phil. 2:17)

--- ∞ ---

How will you live out Life Principle 25 this week? Discuss ways that you can share your gifts and blessings with others. Then spend time in prayer, asking God to draw you into intimate communion with Himself and to transform your life, so that you can affect the world for the sake of His kingdom.

Life Lessons to Remember

❦ *God saved me because He loves me* (see Eph. 1:3–6).

❦ *God's purpose for saving me was to bring Him glory* (see Matt. 5:16).

❦ *I am most like Jesus when I serve others* (see Matt. 20:27–28).

Life Principle 26

Adversity is a bridge to a deeper relationship with God.
Philippians 3:10–11

Life's Questions

There's nothing more lonely than suffering because it feels like no one understands what we're going through. With accomplishments and prosperity, loved ones will gather around to share in our joy and celebrate our success. But with grief, people feel distant, even when they are trying to support and comfort us, because they cannot reach in to that profound place where our pain has made its home. During those times, we may wonder, *Where is God? Why has God allowed this? Has He left me alone to struggle with this by myself? Has God abandoned me?* Yet, just the opposite is true.

Psalm 34:18 assures, "The LORD is near to the brokenhearted and saves those who are crushed in spirit." Adversity isn't a time when God is far from you. On the contrary, it is when He's close to you and teaching you His ways. When everything goes well, you may forget that you need God, but when trouble strikes it's only God who can comfort you to the depth of your soul. He has your full attention and can teach you the joy of His wonderful presence, which is why Life Principle 26 teaches, *Adversity is a bridge to a deeper relationship with God.*

What the Bible Says

Read 2 Corinthians 11:23–31. What did Paul see as validating his ministry (23)?

132

Why does Paul boast in his adversities and infirmities (30)?

Read Philippians 3:3–11. What does Paul say about putting confidence in earthly accomplishments, or "the flesh" (3)?

When Paul writes about the *flesh*, he is speaking of our human nature, our earthly desires and inclinations. Our flesh doesn't follow God. In fact, it's often completely opposed to the Holy Spirit (see Rom. 7). Our flesh seeks carnal pleasures and finds importance in accomplishments, wealth, beauty, and so on. The Spirit, on the other hand, will always direct you to become more like Christ, placing His emphasis on obedience.

Why was Paul content with losing all of his earthly riches and honors (7–8)?

What did Paul find in Christ that he couldn't obtain through possessions and titles (9)?

When Paul set himself to know Christ by faith, what did he find (10–11)?

Why do you think Paul found true life when he was conformed to Christ's death (10–11; also see Mark 10:29–30)?

Read Philippians 3:12–21. What was Paul's goal (12–14; also see 1:13–14, 21–26)?

What happens to those who do not share Paul's focus, but put their trust in earthly accomplishments and wealth (17–19)?

What do adversities prepare us for (20–21)?

What It Means

Paul had everything that defined a successful and blessed life to the people of his time. From birth, he observed the law to the letter and grew to be a very prominent Pharisee. This meant that he had everything that he needed to be right with God and a man of respect in his circle of influence. Paul also enjoyed social prominence. He could trace his lineage to Benjamin, the youngest son of Jacob, and was a descendant of Saul, the first king of Israel. He was born in Tarsus, which gave him all the rights and privileges of a Roman citizen. Very few could match Paul's credentials and accomplishments.

Yet, no matter how pious or perfect he was, it was never enough. Paul needed Jesus. It wasn't through his success that he experienced God, it was through his suffering and adversity. And during those times, God touched him so profoundly and intimately that Paul realized how priceless it was to experience adversity (see Rom. 5:3–5; 8:17–18; 2 Cor. 1:3–11; 12:7–10; Col. 1:24).

―――――――― ∞ ――――――――

I consider that the sufferings of this present time are not worthy to be compared with the glory that is to be revealed to us. (Rom. 8:18)

―――――――― ∞ ――――――――

Life Examples

Read 2 Corinthians 4:5–16. Why has God shone His light in our hearts (5–6)?

What then is the treasure that we have in us as believers (7)?

Why does God allow imperfect people to carry His precious gospel (8–10)?

Living the Principle

Your trials may be prolonged, intense, confusing, complicated, and stressful. At times, you may get frustrated, impatient, and even angry with God. However, the more fiercely you insist on holding on to your earthly sources of pleasure and accomplishment, the longer it will take for God to teach you that only He can heal your soul. And the farther you push Him away and rebel against Him, the more lengthy your time of affliction will be.

The wisest response to your troubles is to surrender your will to God and grow in your relationship with Him. Keep your focus on Him. Trust His love, wisdom, and strength. If you respond the right way, you will know Him more deeply and intimately, and His purpose will be accomplished in you. You will see His glory in a way that you never thought possible.

How will you live out Life Principle 26 this week? Have you experienced God's profound comfort and presence in your life? Discuss the trials that you are facing and how He is reaching deep within your soul to bring you closer to Himself. Then spend time in prayer, asking God to draw you into intimate communion with Himself and to transform your life so that you can affect the world for the sake of His kingdom.

Life Lessons to Remember

* *When adversity strikes, we should immediately turn to God* (see Ps. 40:1–3).

* *Adversity is a tool which God uses to shape His servant for service* (see 1 Peter 1:6–7).

Life Principle 27

$\mathcal{P}$rayer is life's greatest time saver.
2 Thessalonians 3:1

Life's Questions

You wake up knowing that you can't waste a second because there are so many demands on your life. Your heart and mind begin to race. *There just isn't enough time to get it all done,* you tell yourself. As your feet hit the floor, you may be tempted to take off running so that you can engage the frenzy of activity that awaits you. But don't. You need to stop and pray.

Of course, prayer may be one of the things that you've decided to sacrifice to squeeze a few more minutes into your day. You may think, *I'm sorry, God, I just can't stop.* However, understand that you cannot afford to leave God out of your planning. As Life Principle 27 teaches, *Prayer is life's greatest time saver.* If you want to make the most of every moment, you must begin your day with the One who holds every second of your life in His hand.

What the Bible Says

Read 2 Thessalonians 1:3–12. What event is on Paul's mind as he writes to the Thessalonians (7–10)?

What is Paul's prayer for the Thessalonian believers (11–12)?

Read 2 Thessalonians 2:1–7. How would the Thessalonians know that the day of the Lord had arrived (3–4)?

---- ∞ ----

The church at Thessalonica was a young, thriving church that was composed mainly of Gentiles. However, increasing persecution and false teachers who were distorting the truth caused the Thessalonians to worry that they had missed the Second Coming of Christ.

---- ∞ ----

Why do you think God restrains the power of lawlessness (6–7; also see 2 Peter 3:7–9)?

Read 2 Thessalonians 2:8–12. Why do you think God allows the lawless one to be revealed before the Lord destroys him (12; also see Matt. 13:41–43; 24:7–14)?

Read 2 Thessalonians 3:1–5. Knowing that Paul is thinking about the condemnation that awaits the unrighteous (see 2:12), what does he ask from the brethren (1–2)?

Instead of fretting about spreading the gospel to the whole world, what does Paul draw confidence from (3)?

What was Paul counting on concerning other believers (5)?

What It Means

Paul knew Christ's command that believers were to be His witnesses "to the remotest part of the earth" (Acts 1:8). He also realized that, before Christ returns, the "gospel of the kingdom shall be preached in the whole world" (Matt. 24:14). Jesus told the disciples, "There are some of those standing here who will not taste death until they see the kingdom of God" (Luke 9:27). Because the persecution of believers was spreading, many thought that Christ's return was imminent. There was so much to do, so many people to reach and churches to plant, that Paul must have felt overwhelmed by the task, especially with all the obstacles that confronted believers.

However, he knew that God could get it done. If Paul stayed in constant communication with the Lord through prayer, God would maximize his time and give him the wisdom and energy needed to accomplish his part of the mission.

Life Examples

Read Philippians 4:4–7. Why does Paul encourage you to remain calm, gentle, and joyful in the Lord (4–5)?

What are you to do instead of fretting over your troubles (6)?

Why does giving your concerns over to God give you peace (7)?

——— ∞ ———

Certainly God has heard; He has given heed to the voice of my prayer. Blessed be God, who has not turned away my prayer nor His lovingkindness from me. (Ps. 66:19–20)

——— ∞ ———

Living the Principle

Whatever you need to accomplish may seem overwhelming and un-feasible to you. However, "things that are impossible with people are possible with God" (Luke 18:27). God knows everything that will happen to you today, and He knows the best way for you to handle your tasks. Therefore, you must spend time listening to Him in prayer, receiving His wisdom and direction, and drinking in His presence and power. Be quiet before Him, rest in Him, and allow Him to order your steps. He will keep you from moving in the wrong direction or from wasting your time doing useless things. He will slow you down to accomplish the activities that require caution and precision and give you the speed to move through the things that are less important. He will also steer you clear of the time traps you should avoid.

Are you willing to stop and listen to Him? Are you ready for Him to make you as fruitful as you possibly can be? Whether you face a fairly calm day or a day full of activity, commit yourself to His schedule and guidance through prayer. You'll find that your time with God is the best investment that you make every day.

How will you live out Life Principle 27 this week? Discuss times when you've committed your day to God and He accomplished amazing things through you. Then spend time in prayer, asking God to draw you into intimate communion with Himself and to transform your life so that you can affect the world for the sake of His kingdom.

Life Lessons to Remember

🌑 *God will answer our prayers in the way and timing that is absolutely best for us* (see Matt. 21:21–22).

Life Principle 28

No Christian has ever been called to "go it alone" in his or her walk of faith.

Hebrews 10:24–25

Life's Questions

There are many reasons that people don't attend church. Some refuse to join a church because they've had a terrible experience with "religious" people. Others live so far from a biblically-sound congregation that they feel it isn't feasible for them to be active members. At times, people are shy and find it difficult to open up to others, or they have so many responsibilities that they don't think they have the energy to participate adequately. Finally, there are those who are so frightened of being rejected that they isolate themselves from others, including other Christians.

God created each of us for fellowship with Himself and with other believers, which is why Life Principle 28 instructs, *No Christian has ever been called to "go it alone" in his or her walk of faith.* No matter what reason we have for separating ourselves from the Body of Christ, it pales in comparison to why God wants us involved in the church. We need love, encouragement, fellowship, accountability, and a spiritual outlet, and it's through other believers that God provides all those things.

What the Bible Says

Read Acts 6:8–15. What was Stephen accused of?

Read Acts 7:51–60. What did Stephen condemn the Jewish leaders of (51–52)? What did they do to him (58–60)?

Read Acts 8:1–4. What happened after Stephen's death? How did some Christians respond to the persecution (4)?

Many of the believers remained in Jerusalem. What would you have done if you had been in their shoes? Would you have been tempted to go into hiding?

Read Hebrews 10:19–25. Why should believers worship God openly and with great confidence (19–21; also see 4:14–16)?

What is our confidence based on in all situations (23, 35–36)?

Why are we to meet together regularly (24–25; also see 3:12–14)?

—————— ∞ ——————

Stimulate in the New Testament means **to incite** or **stir up.**
We are to encourage and motivate others to be faithful to
God. In the same way, Paul admonished Timothy to "kindle
afresh the gift of God which is in you.... For God has not
given us a spirit of timidity, but of power and love and discipline" (2 Tim. 1:6–7).

—————— ∞ ——————

What It Means

The Jewish community was extremely close knit. They shared ancestry,
land, traditions, and a center of worship. However, when Jews began to
believe in Jesus as their Messiah, they were disowned and persecuted by
their loved ones and neighbors. Some were scattered throughout the
world, while others remained in Jerusalem to weather the storm. All
must have been intensely aware of the persecution that they were in
danger of. Yet the writer of Hebrews admonished them to encourage
one another and remain steadfast in their faith (see Heb. 3:13).

They needed to draw confidence from other believers, and so do you,
especially during the most difficult times. Other Christians will help
you grow in your faith, and they will give you the love and support that
you need to face the challenges ahead.

Life Examples

Read 1 John 3:13–19. Why should we not be surprised when the
world opposes us (13; also see John 15:17–19)?

How does our unconditional love for one another show that we belong
to Christ and are saved (14; also see 1 John 4:7–11)?

When we refuse to show love to other believers, why is it a condemnation against us (14–15; also see 1 John 4:20–21)?

What should we be willing to do for other believers (16; also see John 15:13)? What impact does this have on our opinions, prejudices, and biases?

What does this passage admonish about sharing with those in need (17–19; also see James 2:15–17)?

Love one another, even as I have loved you ... By this all men will know that you are My disciples, if you have love for one another (John 13:34–35).

Living the Principle

Do you find it easy or difficult to open up to other people? Do you consider yourself a loner or are you naturally drawn to others? Regardless of your personal makeup, you need to understand how important it is for you to be part of the church. This will be more challenging for some than for others, but being involved in a Bible-believing congregation is indispensable for *all* Christians. Bombarded by worldly pressure and ungodly influences, no one can stand by themselves for too long. Either you will be destroyed by the stress or you will drift away from the faith. Also, you will miss out on the abundant life that God planned for you because an important part of expressing that life is showing unconditional love to other believers and receiving it from them in return. That's not possible if you refuse to participate.

Are you involved in a local church? If you're not, you need to be. Make sure that you attend a church that will encourage you, keep you accountable, challenge you to grow, help you to express your spiritual gifts, and feed you the meat of God's Word. Remember, the Body of Christ isn't complete without you, so don't wait any longer to fulfill the role that you were created for.

How will you live out Life Principle 28 this week? Discuss your involvement in the local church and encourage each other in your service for the Lord. Then spend time in prayer, asking God to draw you into intimate communion with Himself and to transform your life so that you can affect the world for the sake of His kingdom.

Life Lessons to Remember

🌵 *Meeting regularly with other believers helps to safeguard us against drifting* (see Heb. 3:13).

🌵 *We have a responsibility to use our gifts to encourage other believers* (see 1 Peter 4:10).

Life Principle 29

We learn more in our valley experiences than on our mountaintops.

James 5:10

Life's Questions

Perhaps you've noticed that many of the Life Principles are focused on how you respond to adversity. This is because of the precept found in Life Principle 29: *We learn more in our valley experiences than on our mountaintops.*

God often leads us through difficult times to teach us. Of course, you may be disheartened while staring up at the obstacles that surround you. Your challenges may be so immense and your choices so limited that you feel weak, completely unable to crawl out of the valley. You may even be tempted to think, *Is this it? Is this all there is? Is this the end of my story?*

If that's the case, then be encouraged. This is *not* the end of your story. Things *will* change because God's will for you is "good and acceptable and perfect" (Rom. 12:2). However, right now, there is something that God wants you to learn. Consider how He is working in your life. What is God teaching you through this valley?

What the Bible Says

Read James 1:1–8. To whom is this letter written (1)?

--------------- ∞ ---------------

James is writing to the Jewish Christians that were described in Life Principle 28, who were driven from Jerusalem by the persecution of the Jewish authorities (see Acts 8:1–4). They were away from their homes and families, and not welcomed by their new communities.

--------------- ∞ ---------------

Why were these brethren to be joyful in their trials (2–3)?

Why is endurance such an important characteristic (4)?

How can believers remain patient in difficult situations (5; also see Prov. 2:2–8)?

Read James 5:7–11. What are believers to look forward to (7)?

Why do you think grumbling against others increases when we're under pressure (9)?

How can we avoid complaining when we're in a difficult situation (9)?

Why is remembering the prophets—such as Moses, Samuel, Isaiah, Habakkuk, and so on—encouraging to us (10–11; also see Rom. 15:4)?

--- ∽ ---

*S*ometimes God allows us to go without any earthly or human comfort so that we will turn completely to Him.

--- ∽ ---

What It Means

There are two words in the New Testament for *patience*. The first has to do with difficult circumstances and means to *stay the course* or *endure*. The second is more personal because it has to do with how we relate to other people. It means *to stay away from rage or furious outbursts*. The believers that James was writing to could have gotten angry and struck out at their persecutors. They were even beginning to turn on one another. However, James admonished them to be patient and trust God. He wrote, "We count those blessed who endured ... the Lord is full of compassion and is merciful" (James 5:11).

Is your trial exposing areas of anger, bitterness, or unforgiveness in your life? Are you finding it difficult to persevere because you don't

trust God with certain issues? Then you are starting to understand what He wants you to learn through your trial. Remember, you will be blessed if you endure. Therefore, embrace what He's teaching you.

Life Examples

Read James 5:13–16. How do your trials help you grow closer to others and to God?

Read 1 Kings 17:1 and 18:1. How long did the land go without rain?

Read 1 Kings 18:41–45. What did Elijah say would happen (41)?

Then what did Elijah do (41–42)?

Read James 5:17–18. Why does knowing that Elijah is just like you help you when you're in the valley?

Living the Principle

Anytime that you experience adversity, it is because God wants to show you His power and love. He may be getting your attention to free you from some emotional bondage or destructive habits. There may be an attitude or behavior in your life that is hindering His work, and He needs to eliminate it. Perhaps there is some precious quality that He wants to develop in you.

Whatever the reason for the trial, God never means it for your harm. Rather, He means it for your good so you can become everything that you were created to be and experience His abundant blessings. Therefore, respond in the way that honors Him. Stay close to Him in prayer and through His Word, obeying whatever He tells you to do. Learn through your valley experiences so that God can prepare you for the mountaintops because your story is not over. The best is still to come.

How will you live out Life Principle 29 this week? Discuss the valleys that you've been experiencing and what God is teaching you through them. Then spend time in prayer, asking God to draw you into intimate communion with Himself and to transform your life so that you can affect the world for the sake of His kingdom.

Life Lessons to Remember

🌿 *Adversity gets our attention* (see Ps. 77:2).

🌿 *Adversity leads to examination* (see Ps. 77:6-12).

🌿 *Adversity leads to a change in behavior* (see Ps. 119:67).

Life Principle 30

An eager anticipation of the Lord's return keeps us living productively.

Revelation 22:12

Life's Questions

What would you do if you knew that Jesus was returning in just a few hours? Would you be happy and prepare for the celebration? Or would you want to clean up some aspects of your life?

———— ∞ ————

When the Lord returns in all His glory, will He find you eager to see Him?

———— ∞ ————

The Second Coming of Christ should be a joyous time for all believers. After all, 1 Thessalonians 4:16–17 tells us, "The Lord Himself will descend from heaven with a shout ... Then we who are alive and remain will be caught up together with them in the clouds to meet the Lord in the air, and so we shall always be with the Lord." When the Lord returns, He is coming to take you to your new home in heaven, to the place that He has prepared especially for you (see John 14:1–3). It is going to be a wonderful time and you don't want any regrets to taint your happy reunion with the Lord. That's why Life Principle 30 admonishes, *An eager anticipation of the Lord's return keeps us living productively.*

What the Bible Says

Read Matthew 24:36–44. Does anyone know when Jesus will return (36)?

How did Noah know that the flood was coming (37–39; also see Gen. 6:13–22)? Who else knew?

What kinds of activities will people be doing when the Son of God returns (40–41)?

Why should you be watchful for Christ's return, even though you don't know when He is coming (42–44)?

Read Matthew 24:45–51. What happened to the servant who was hard at work preparing for the master's return (45–47)?

Whom do you need to warn about the consequences of ignoring the Lord's return (50–51)?

——————— ∞ ———————

$\mathcal{A}$t the Great White Throne Judgment (see Rev. 20:11–15), everyone is judged according to whether or not they've accepted Christ as their Savior. Those who have not will be cast into the lake of fire. Those who have been redeemed will be welcomed into heaven. However, believers will also face an assessment of their works at the judgment seat of Christ (see 1 Cor. 3:11-15; 2 Cor. 5:9–10).

——————— ∞ ———————

What It Means

You may be thinking, *Even during Jesus' time, they thought that He was going to return quickly. The Lord's return is probably a lot farther off than we think. We have plenty of time.* However, that is an extremely unwise way to live. You have no idea when God will call you home to heaven, by His return or by some other means. You also don't know when He will require the souls of your loved ones (see Luke 12:20). None of us are promised tomorrow (see James 4:13–15). You always need to remember that you may see the Lord at any minute because that can keep you motivated to serve Him with all of your heart, mind, soul, and strength.

Life Examples

Read Revelation 22:1–5. What will heaven be like (1–2)? What will believers do there (3–5)?

Read Revelation 22:6–21. Does this passage of Scripture anticipate a long or short amount of time before the Lord returns (6–7)? Could Jesus return *today*?

What is Christ's promise to those who serve Him faithfully (12–14)?

Who will be excluded from heaven (15)? Do you know anyone who will be locked out?

——————— ∞ ———————

*N*othing unclean, and no one who practices abomination and lying, shall ever come into it, but only those whose names are written in the Lamb's book of life. (Rev. 21:27)

——————— ∞ ———————

You are the church, the *bride* of Christ. Have you bid everyone to "Come!' ... let the one who is thirsty come ... take the water of life without cost" (17)?

What will your reaction be when Christ returns (20)?

Living the Principle

Christ's Second Coming should not be just a far off hope for you. It should be a daily reminder that God is *always* active in your life. God leaves you on earth after you are saved for two main reasons: One is to grow spiritually in oneness with Him; the second is to lead others to a saving knowledge of Jesus Christ. Is that what you've been busy doing? Have you been seeking and serving Him, remembering the reward that awaits you? It's good to keep His return at the forefront of your mind so that, when you do finally meet Jesus, you can be just as glad to see Him as He is to see you.

Therefore, be motivated! Rejoice! Live your life to the fullest and set your eyes and heart firmly on the promise of Christ's return. He's prepared a great reward and a wonderful home for you in heaven. Be strong—diligently working and expectantly watching—because one day, probably sooner than you expect, you are going to see Him face to face.

How will you live out Life Principle 30 this week? Discuss how you feel about the Second Coming of Christ. Celebrate His presence with each other. Talk about how you can watch for His return and live faithful lives that will please Him. Then spend time in prayer, asking God to draw you into intimate communion with Himself and to transform your life so that you can affect the world for the sake of His kingdom.

Life Lessons to Remember

🌱 *We are to watch for the Lord's return* (see Ezek. 33:7; Mark 13:32–33).

🌱 *We are to work as if the Lord were returning soon* (see Matt. 9:37–38; 24:45–47).

🌱 *We are to eagerly anticipate the Lord's return* (see Isa. 62:11–12).